I0390645

A

Birder's

Collection

Book 2

By RJ & IrisBenjamina
Chris Johnson Nature Photography

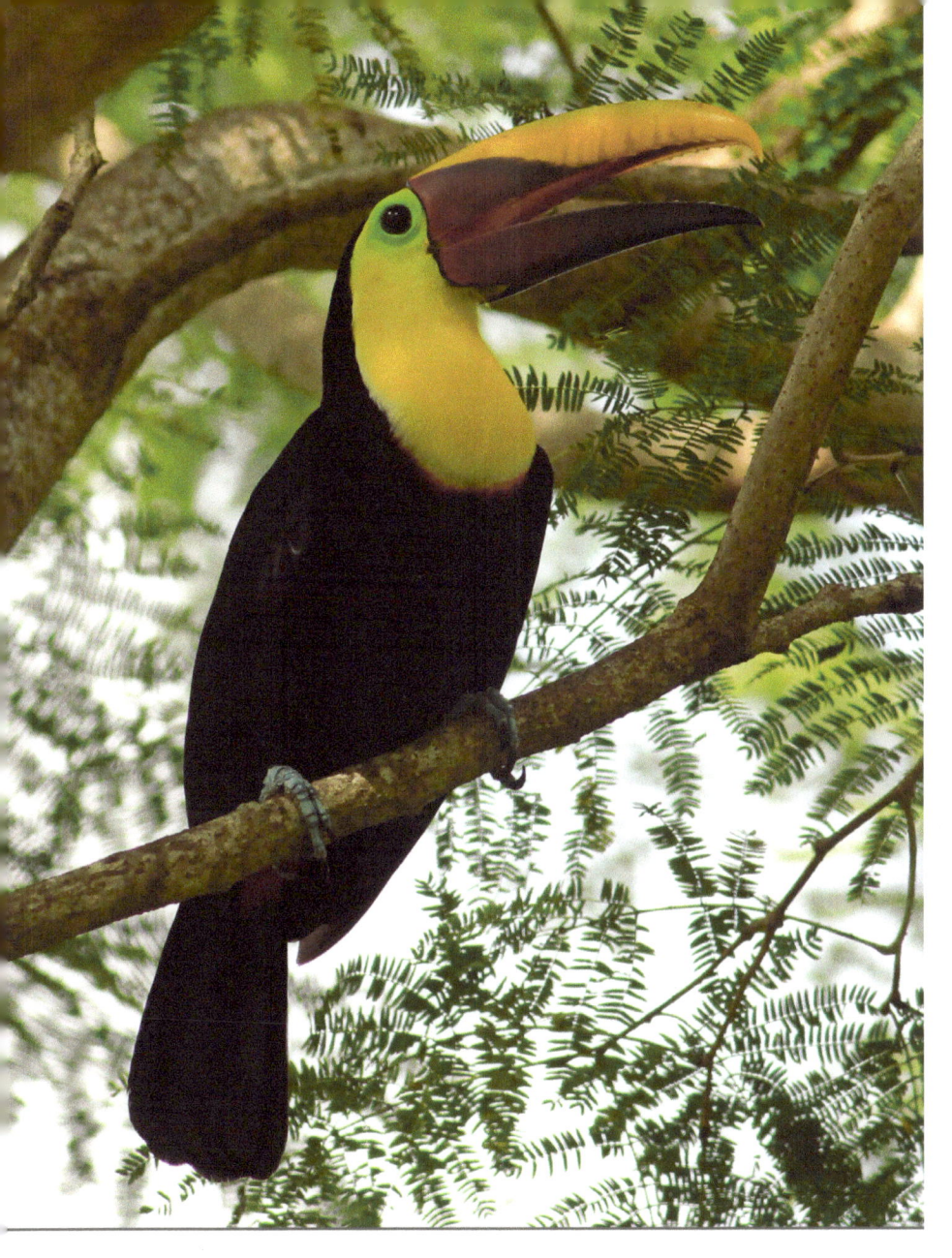

Chestnut-mandibled Toucan

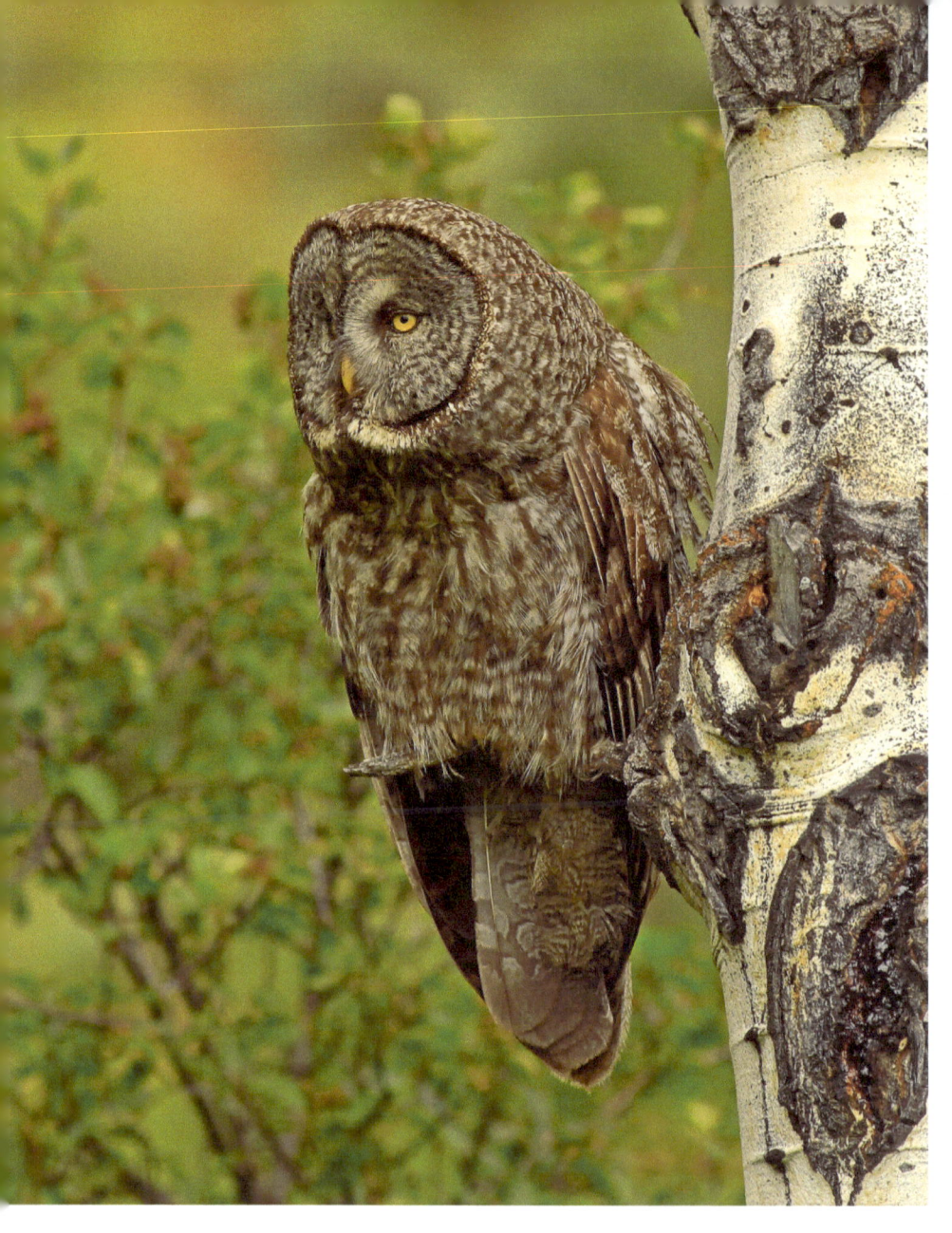

Great-gray Owl

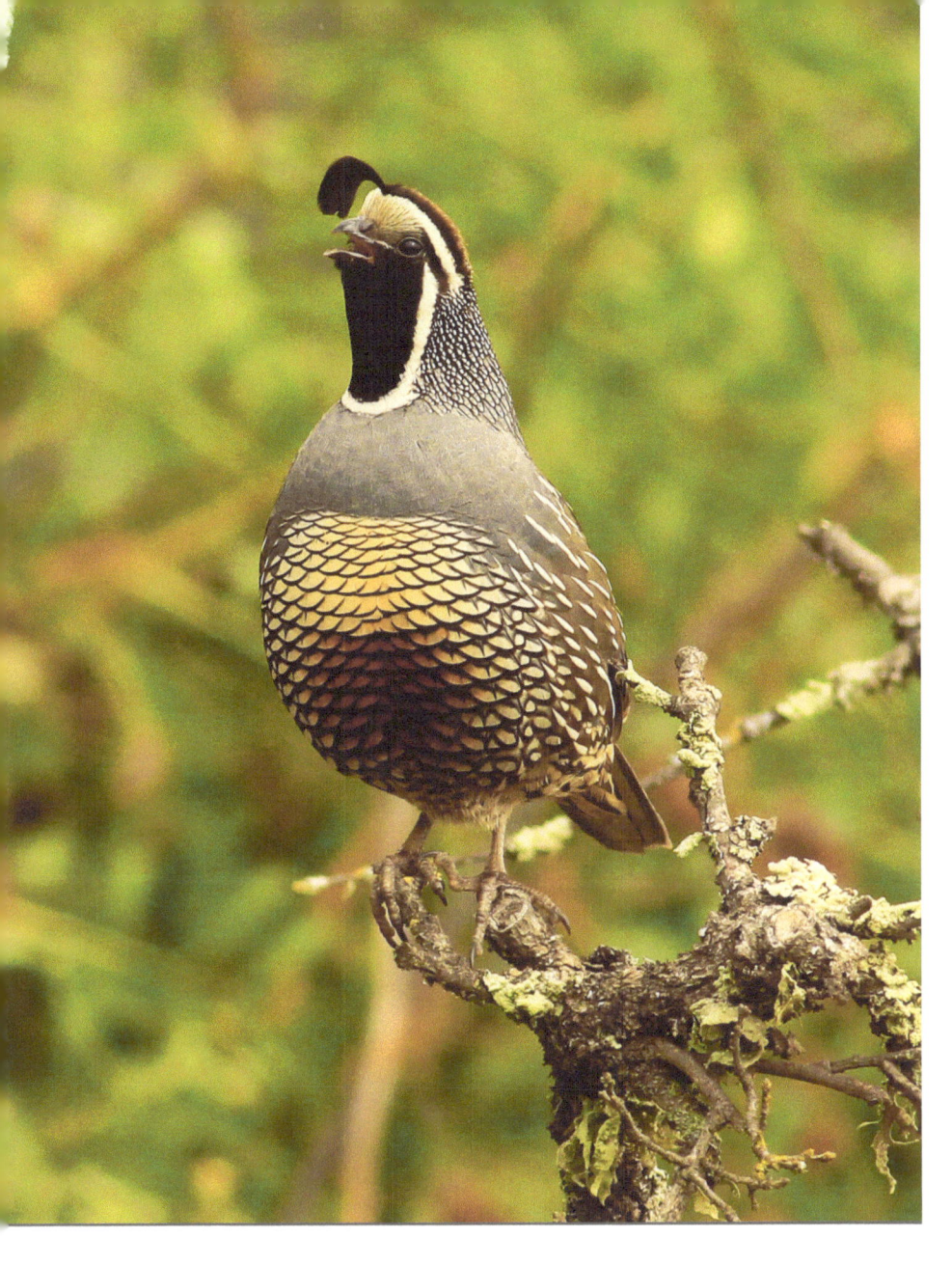

Great-gray Owl

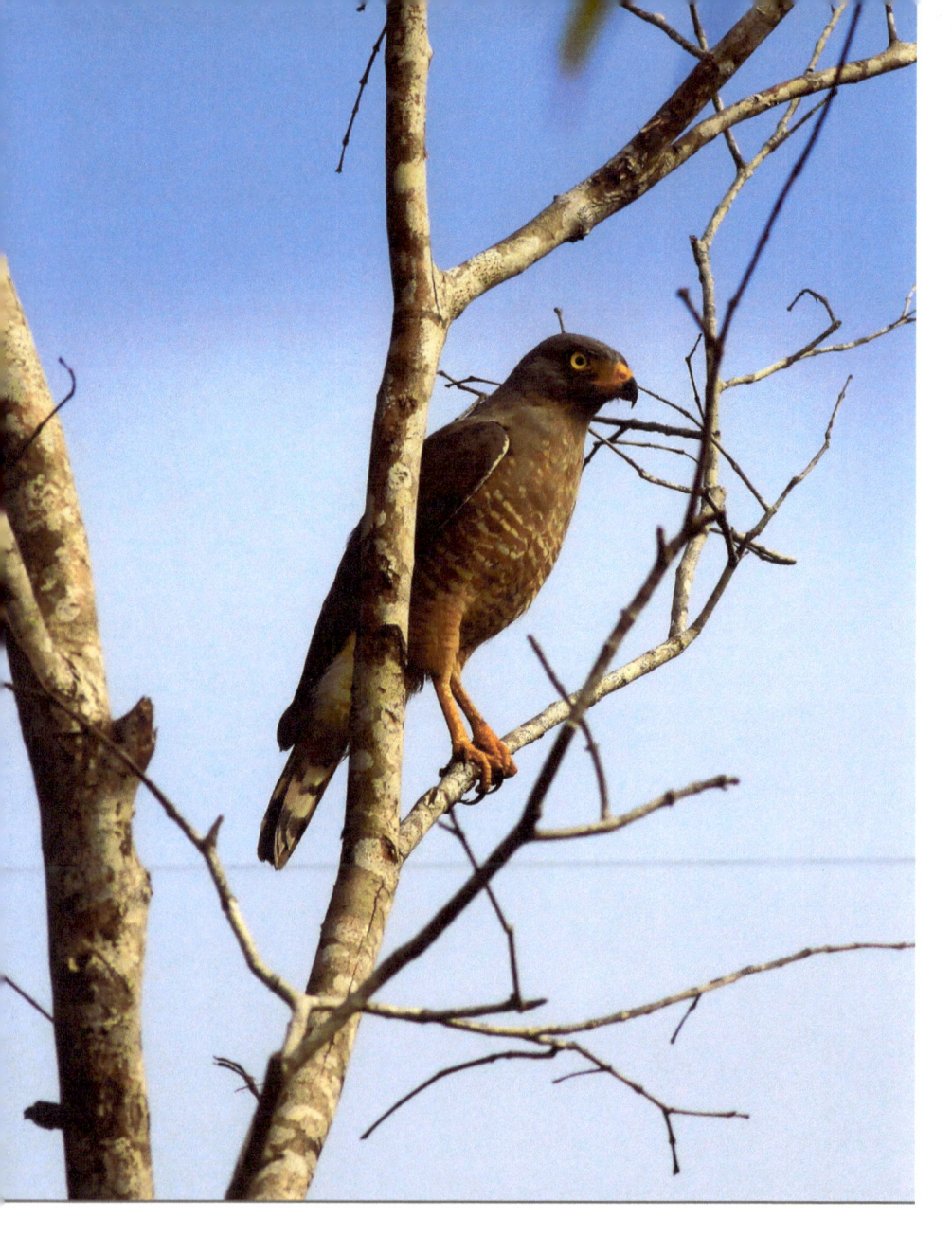

Roadside Hawk

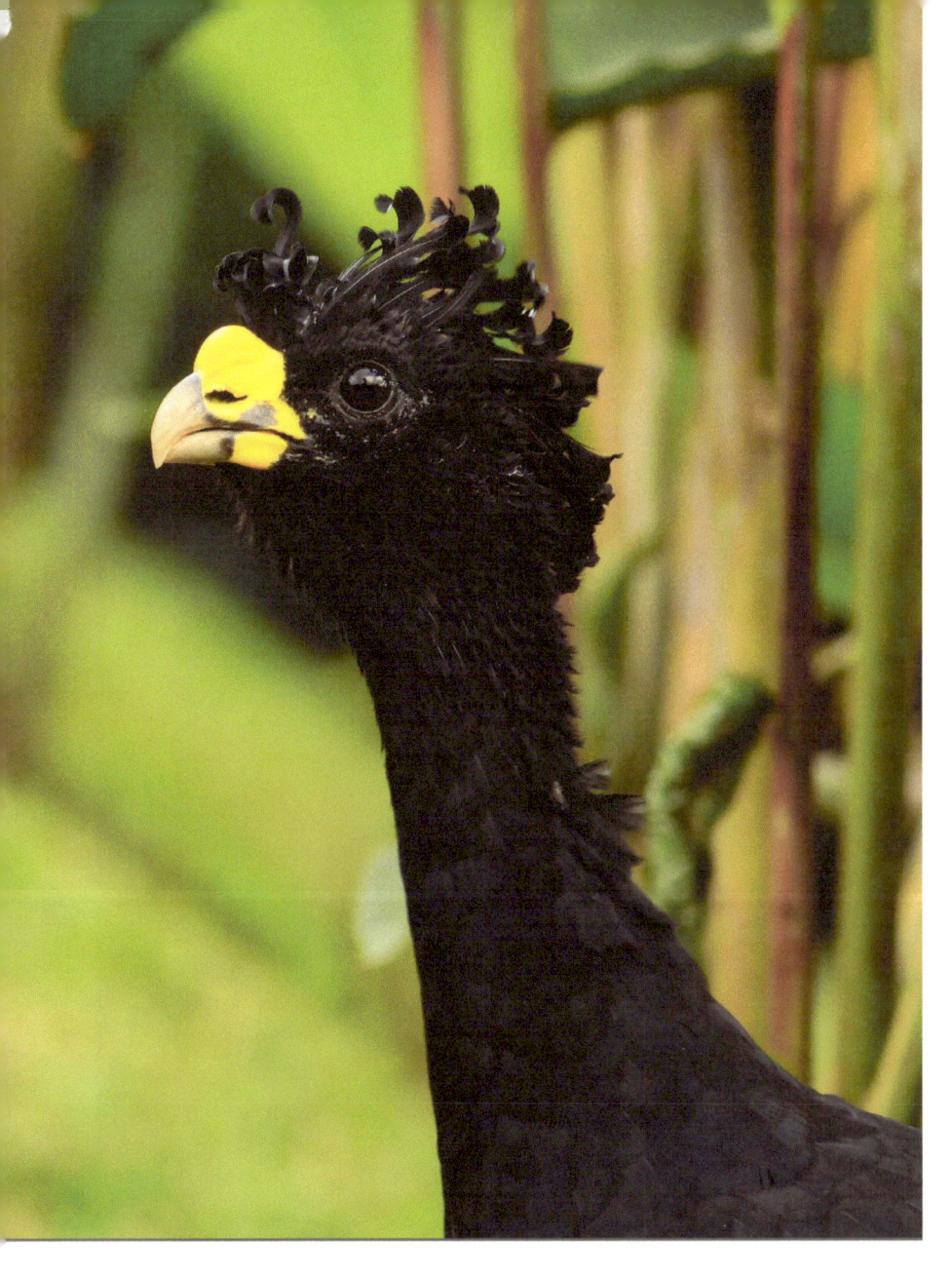

Giant Currasow

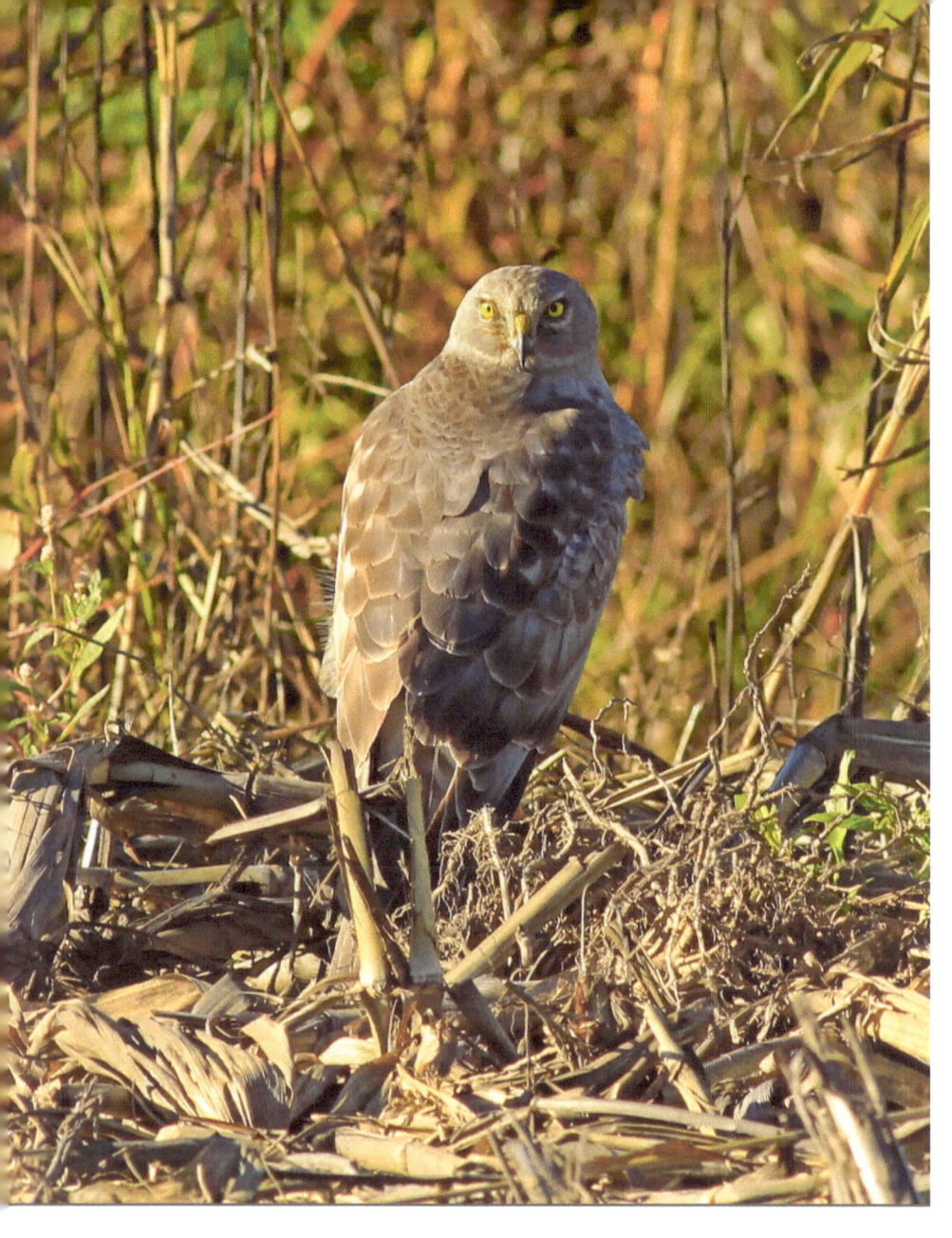

Northern Harrier male

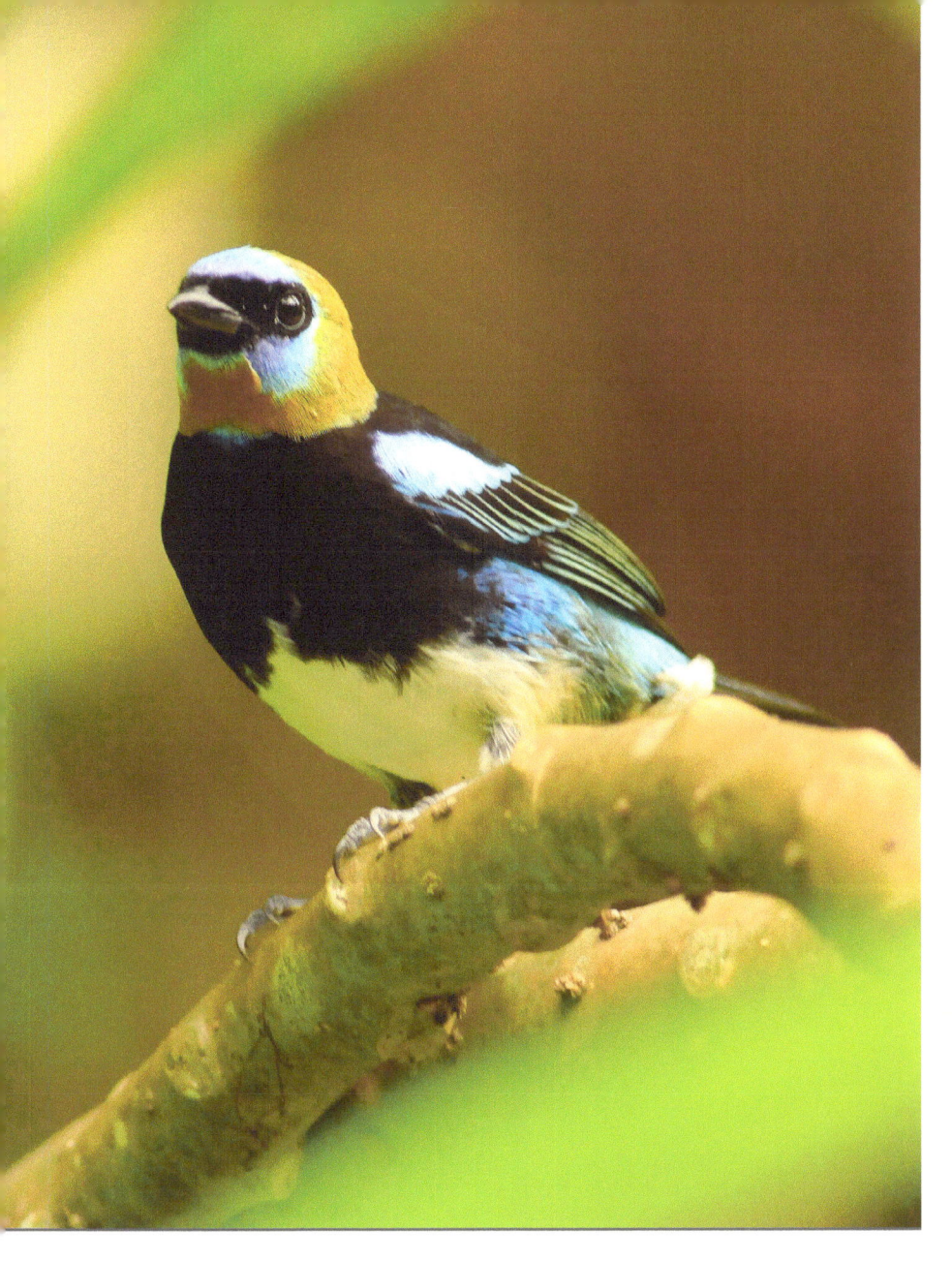

Golden-hooded Tanager

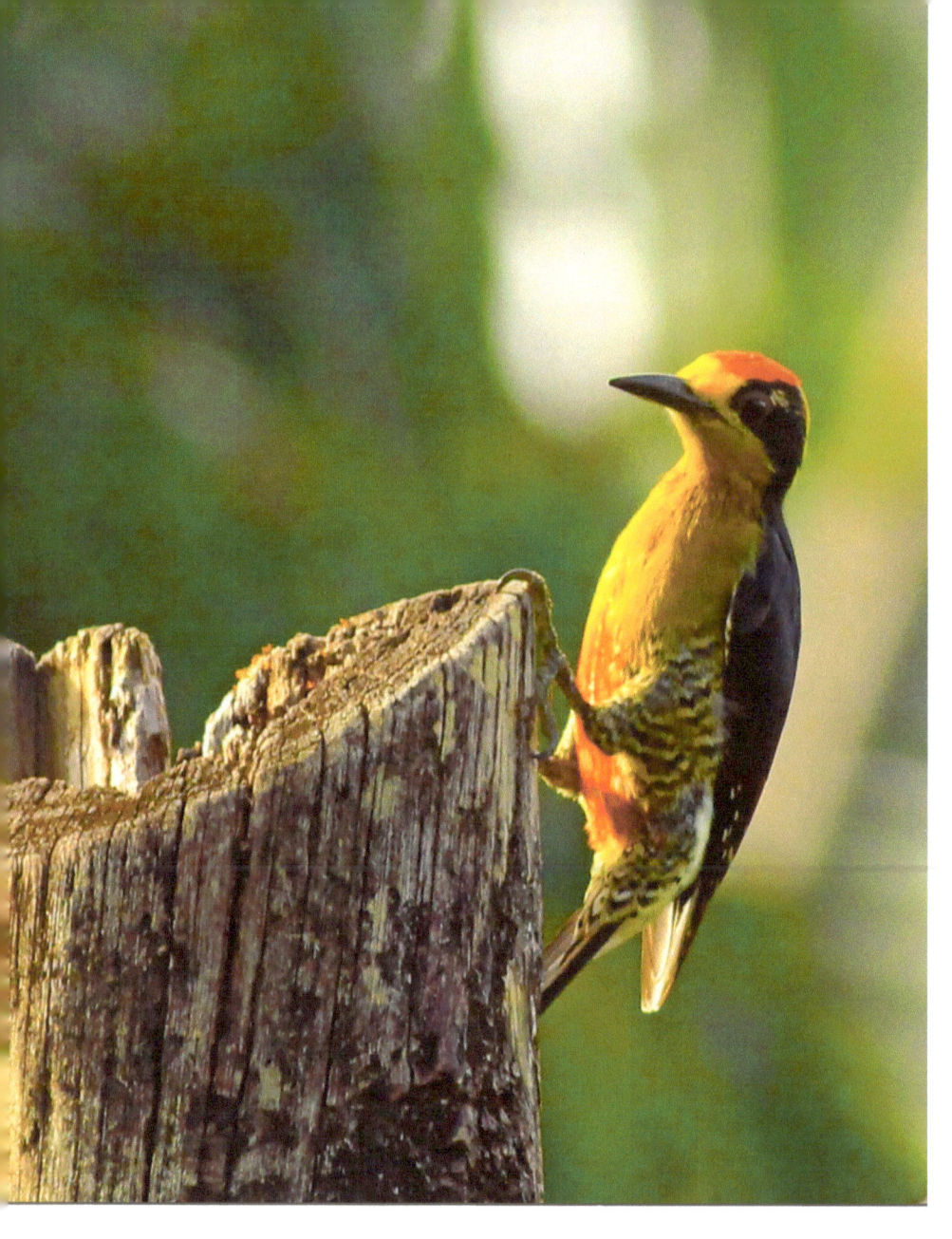

Golden-naped Woodpecker

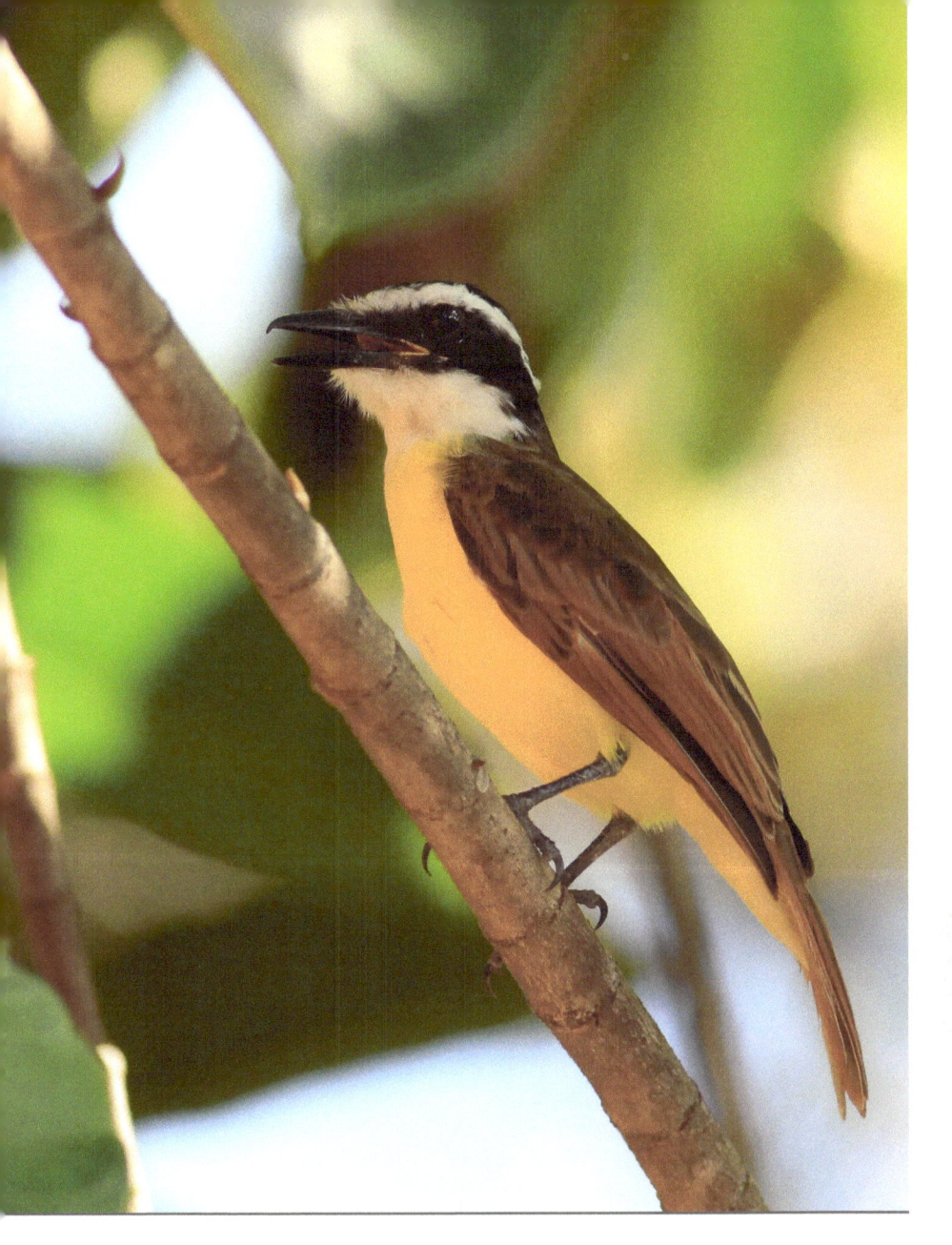

Great Kiskadee,

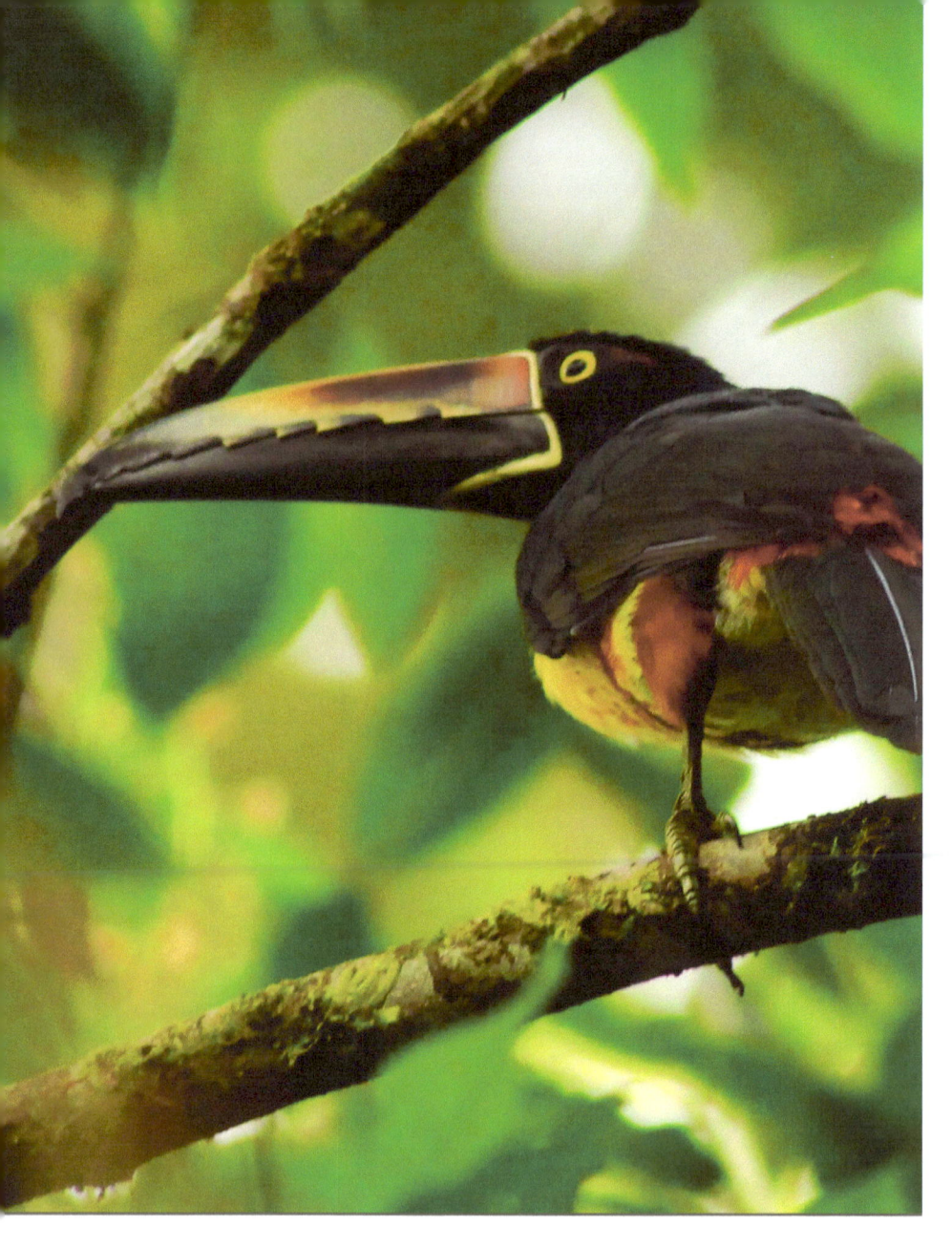

Fiery-billed Aracari

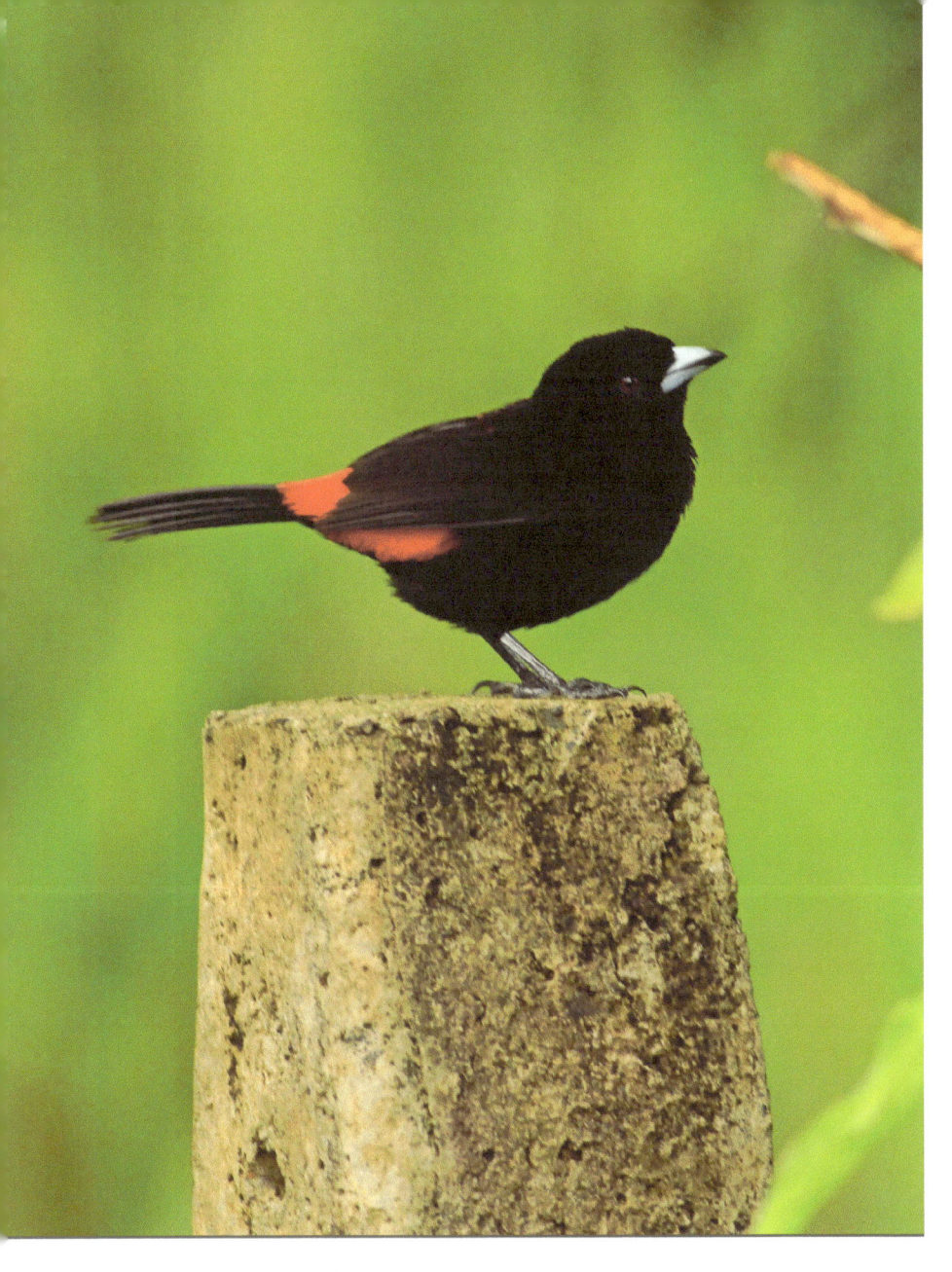

Scarlet-rumped Passerini's Tanager

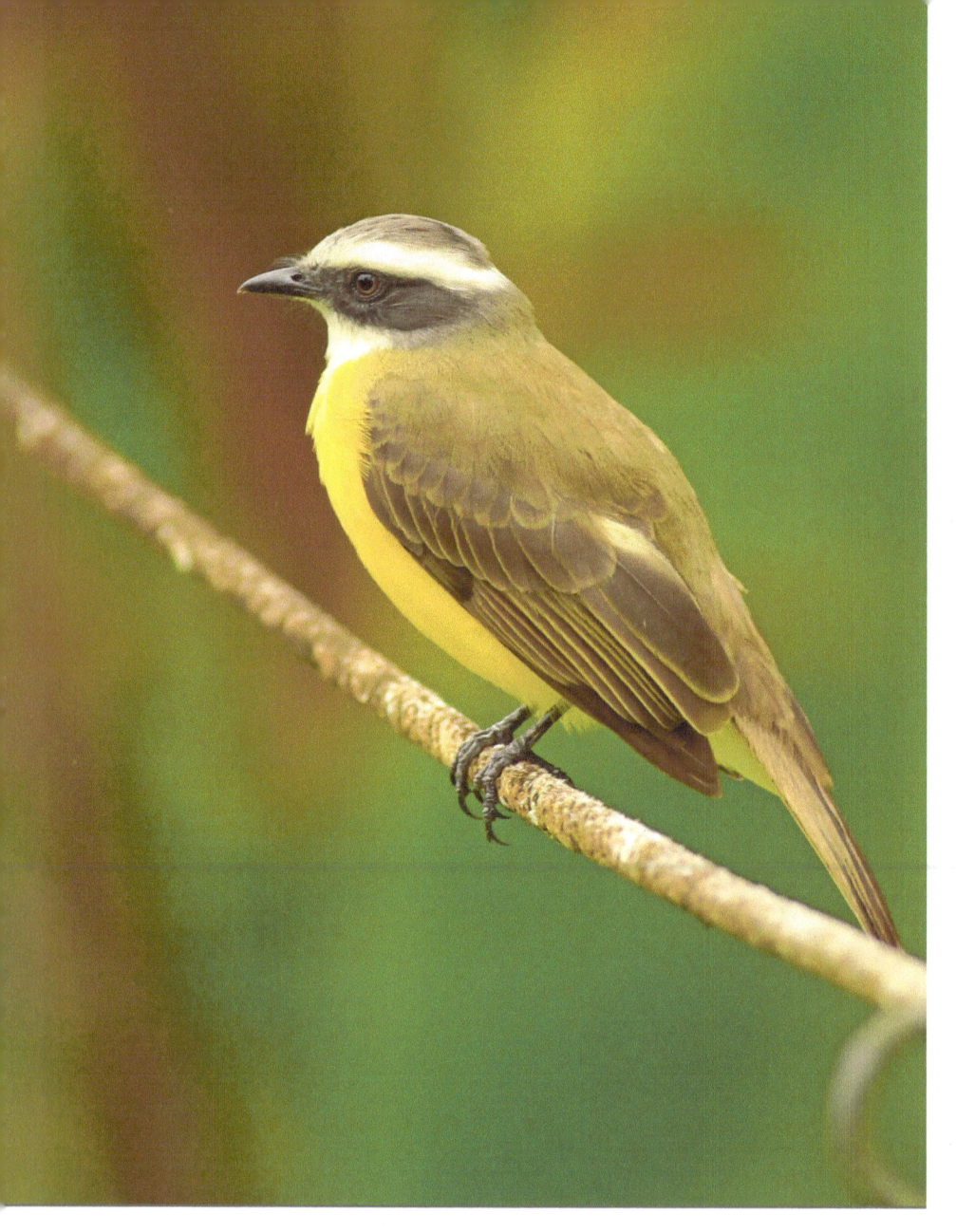

White-ringed Flycatcher

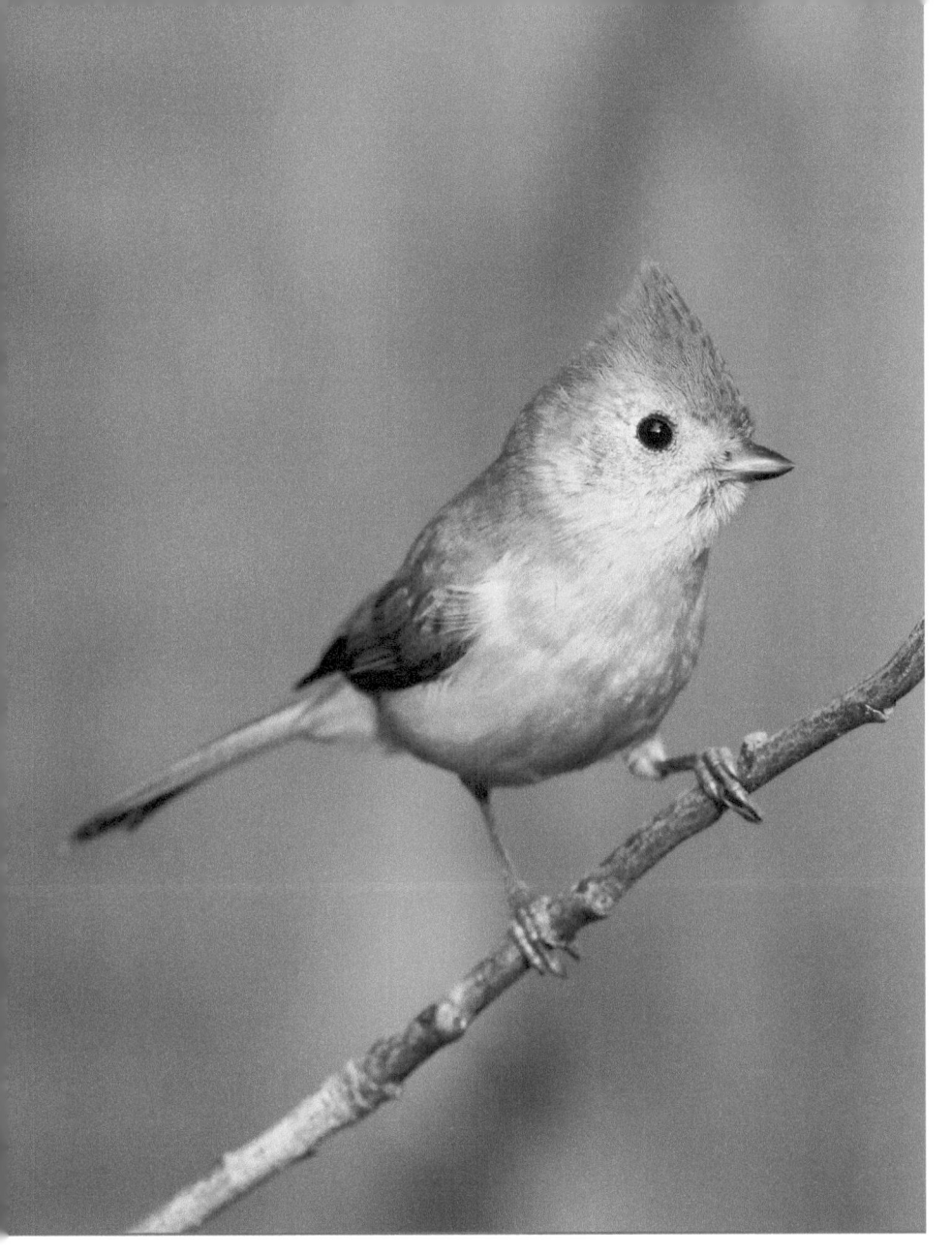

Titmouse

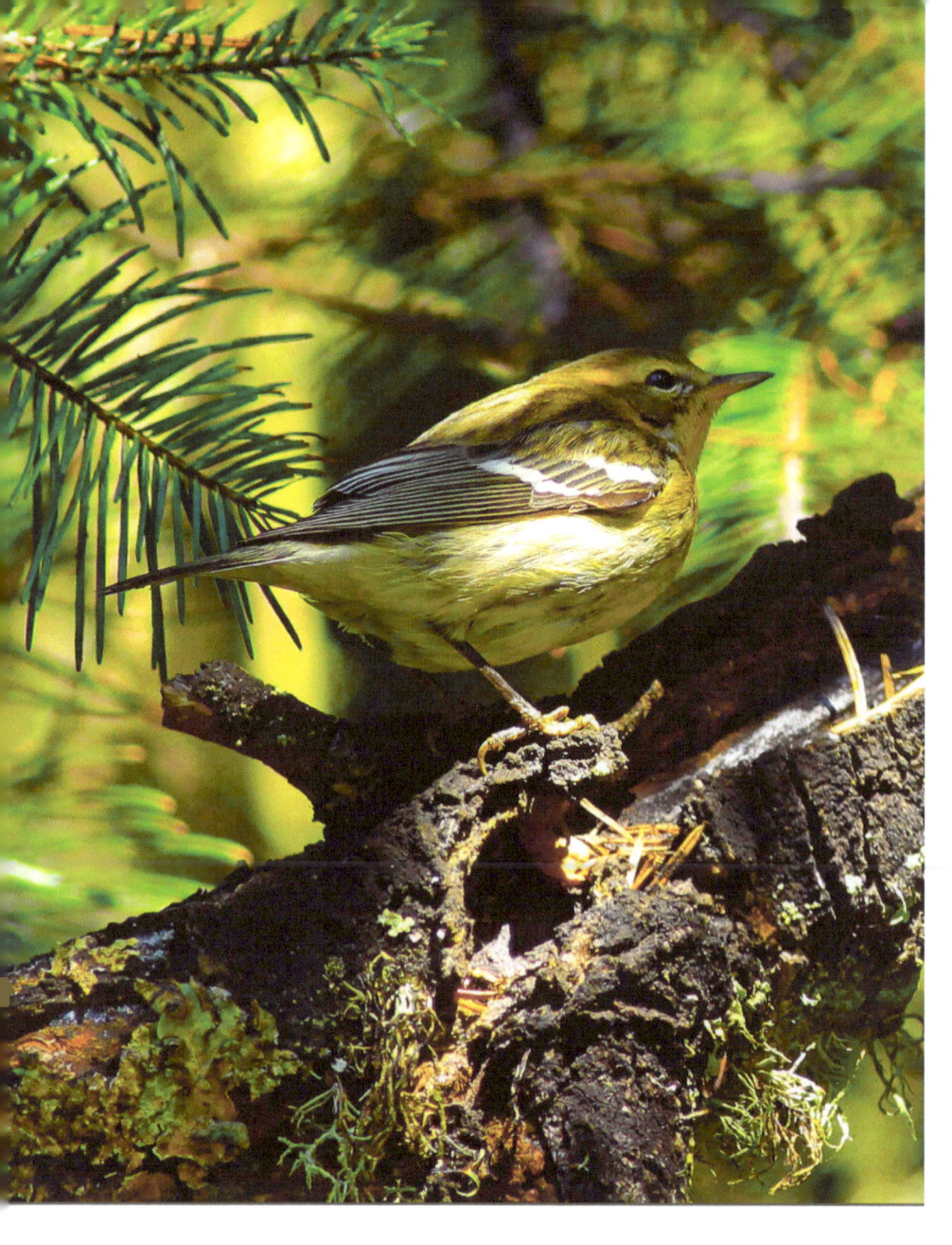

Blackburnian Warbler

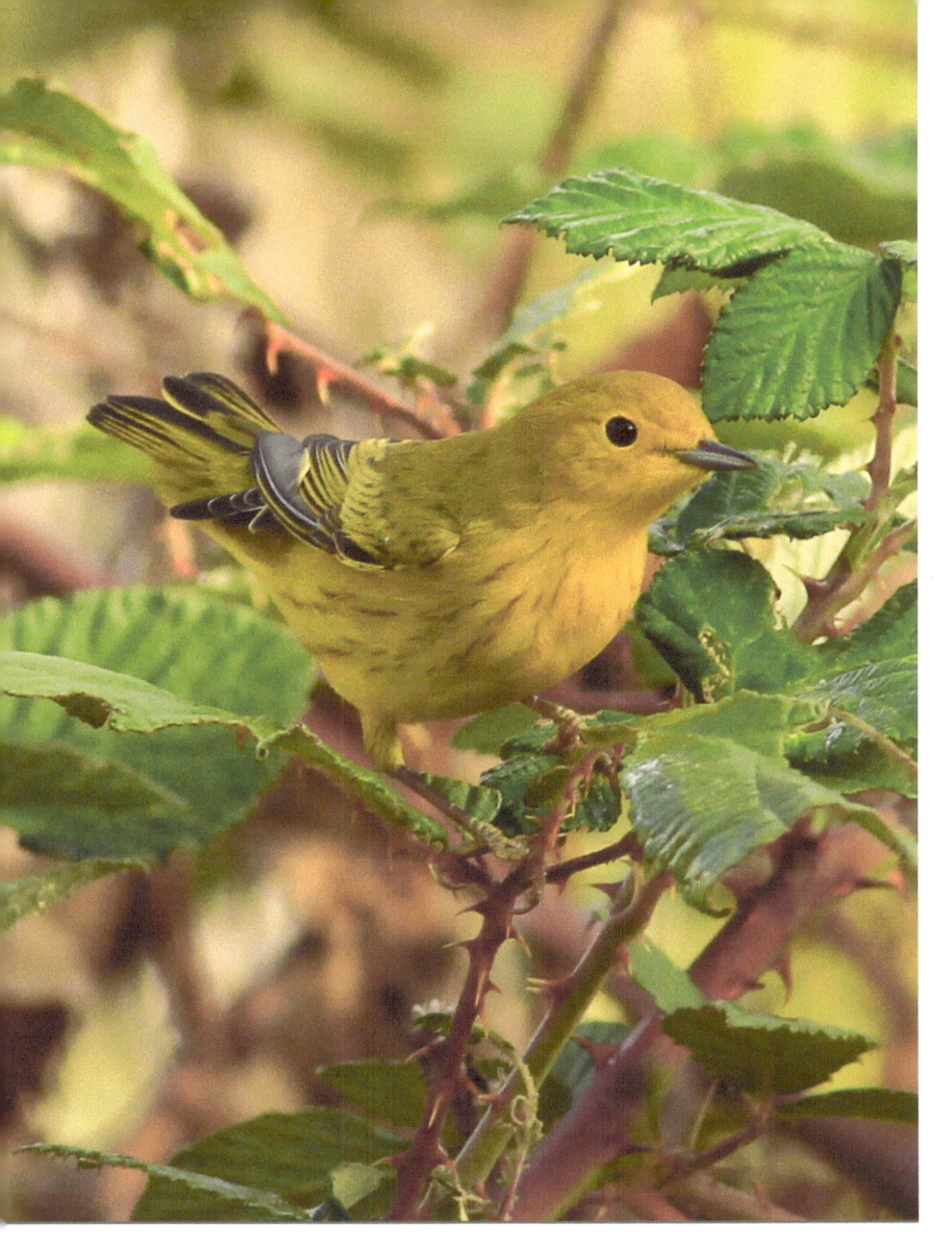

Yellow Warbler male

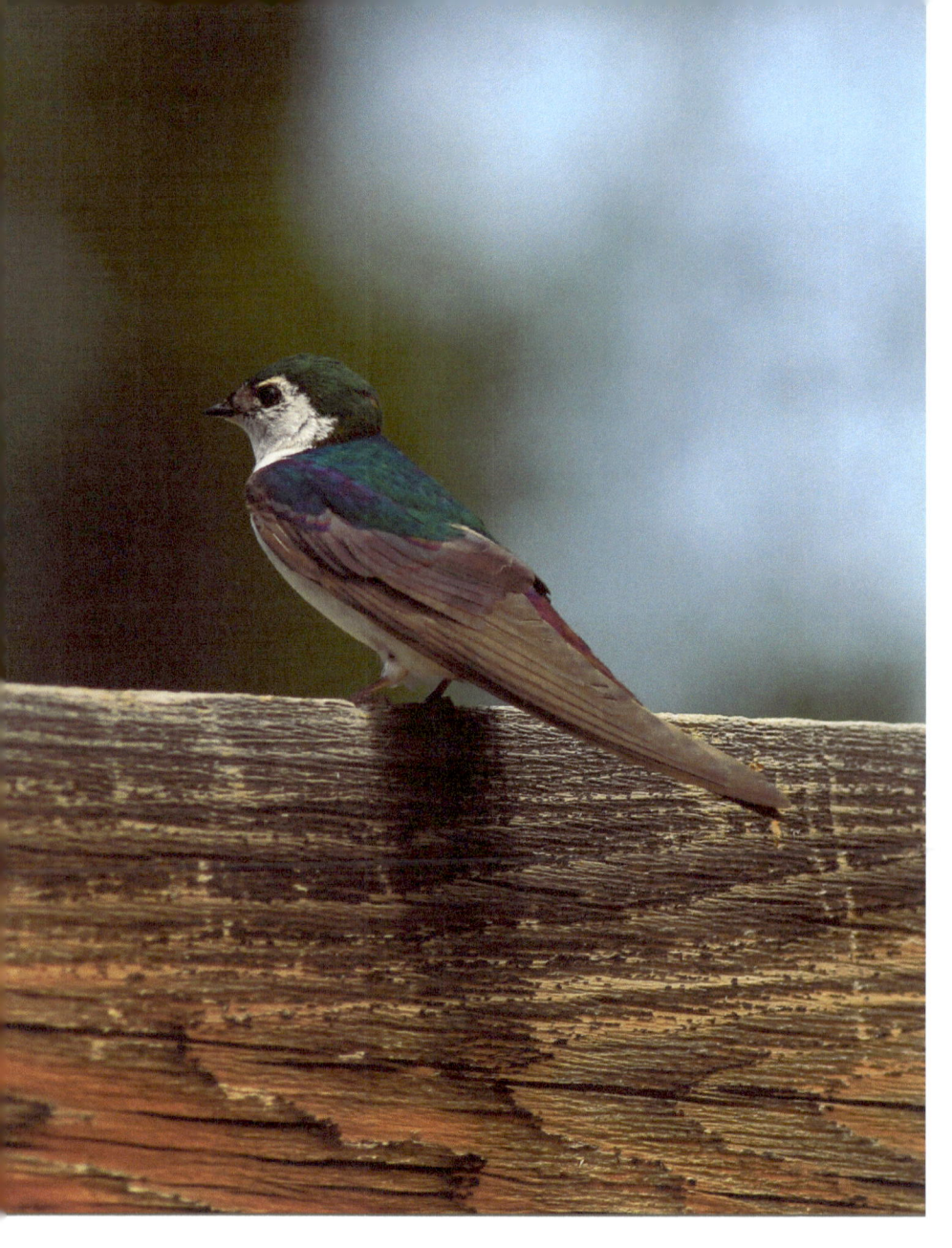

Violet-green Tree Swallow

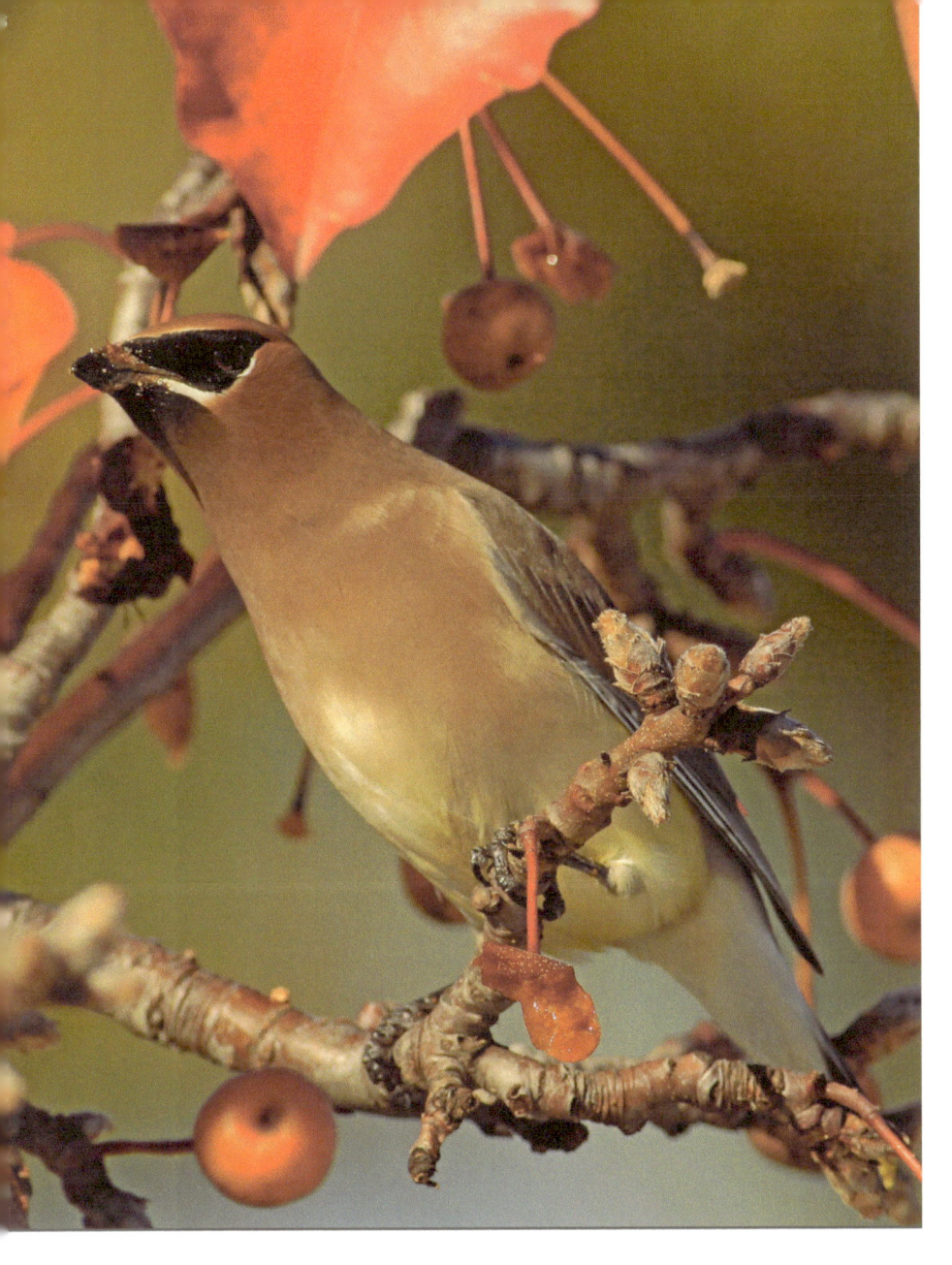

Cedar Waxwing

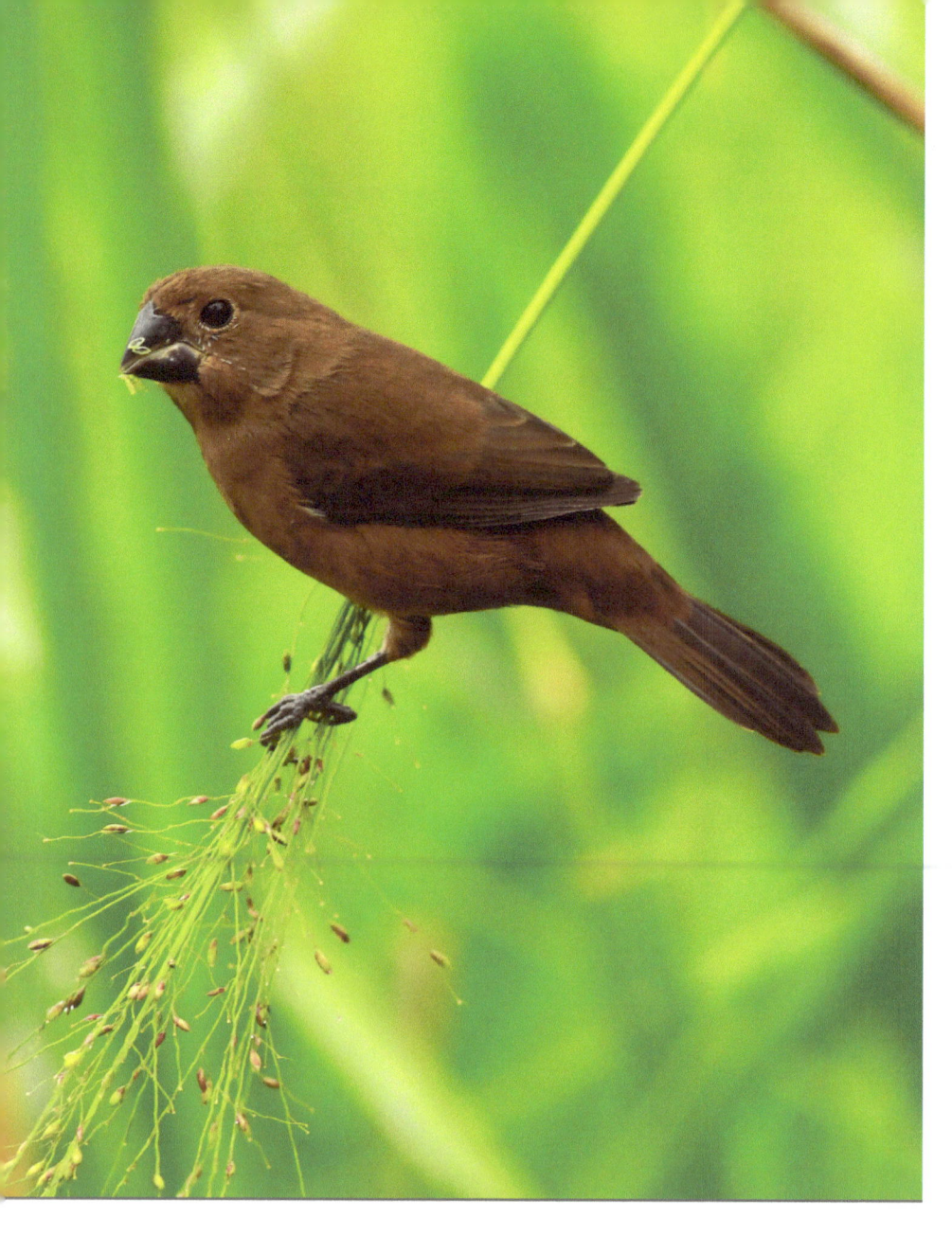

Thick-billled Seed-finch

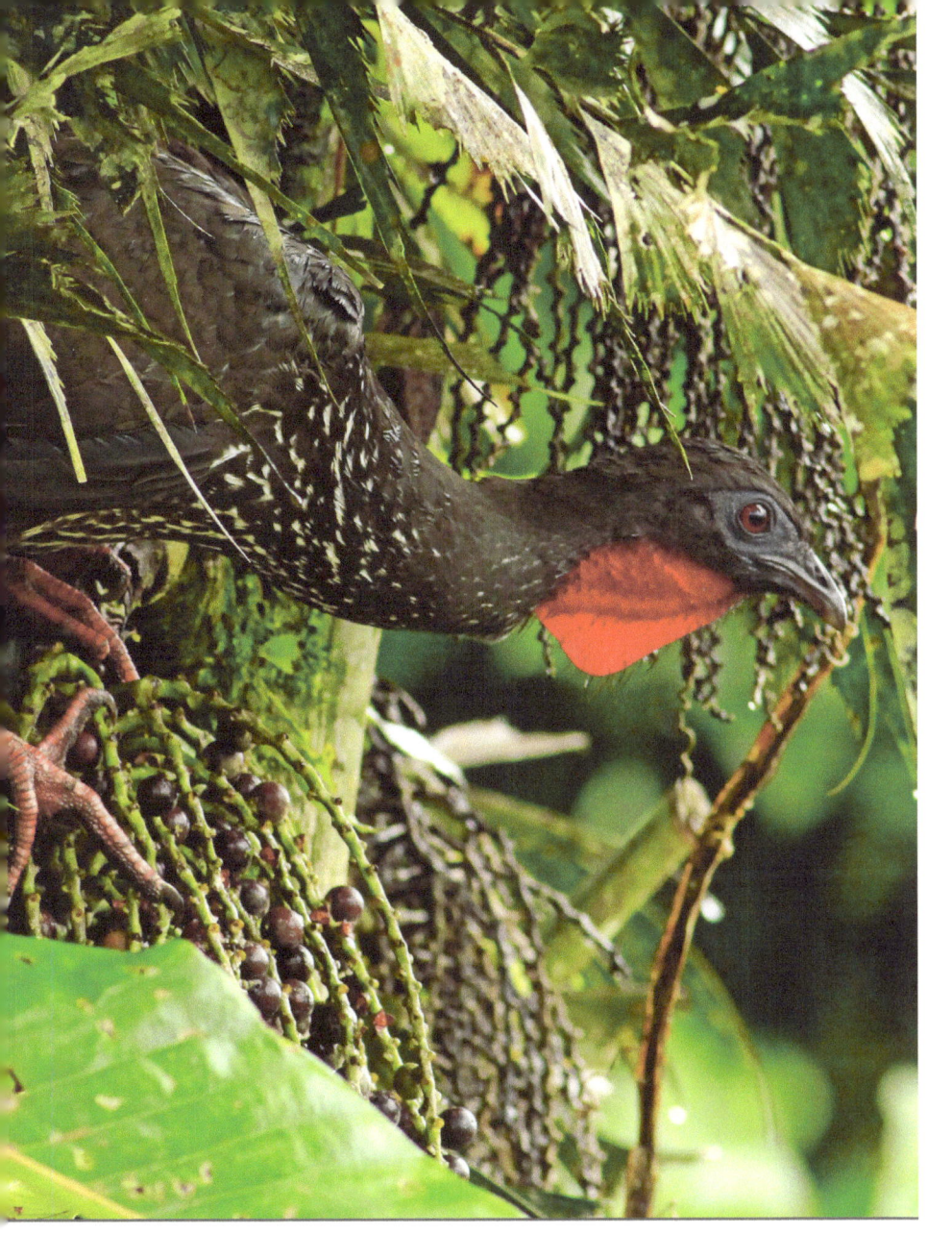

Crested Guan

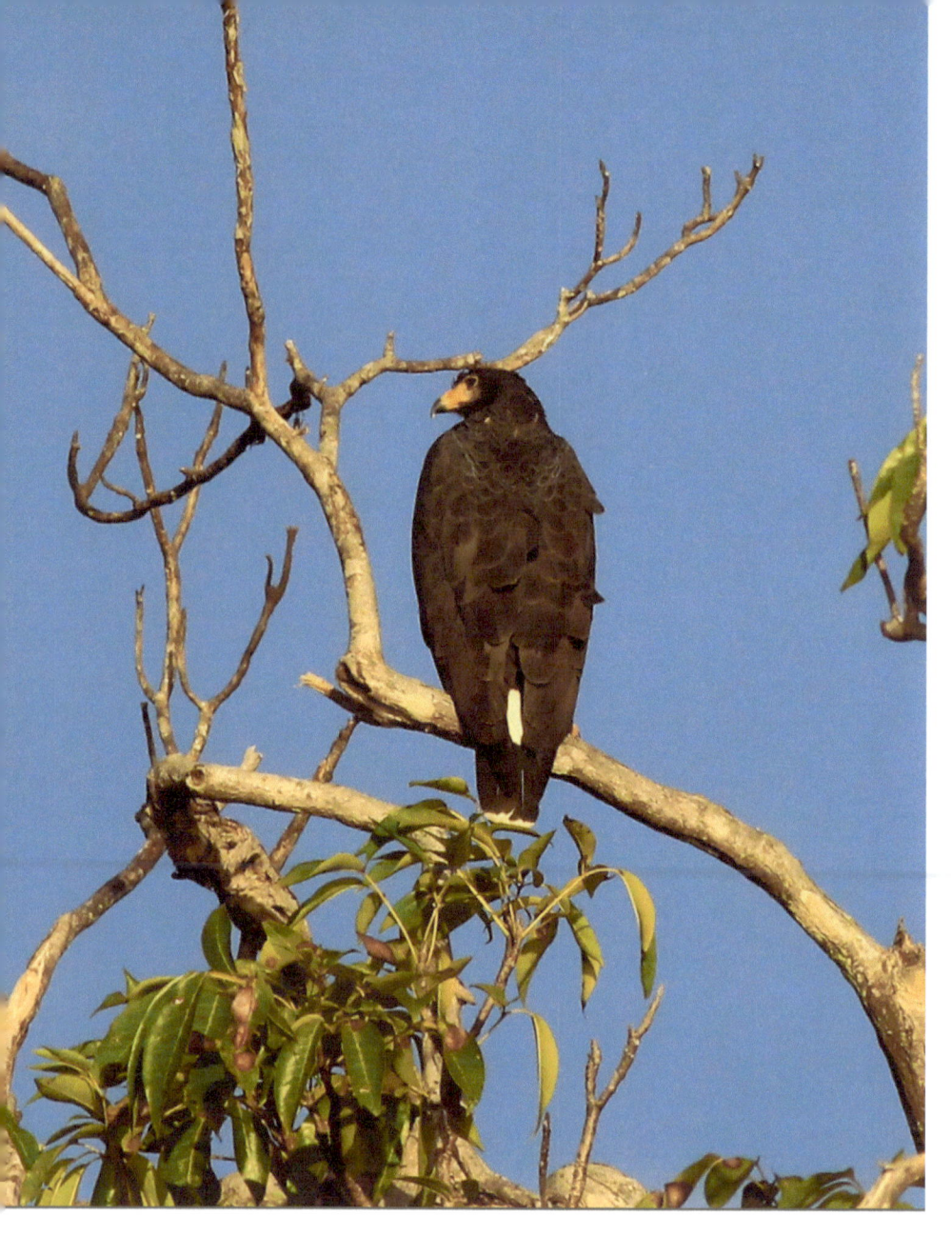

Mangrove Black-Hawk

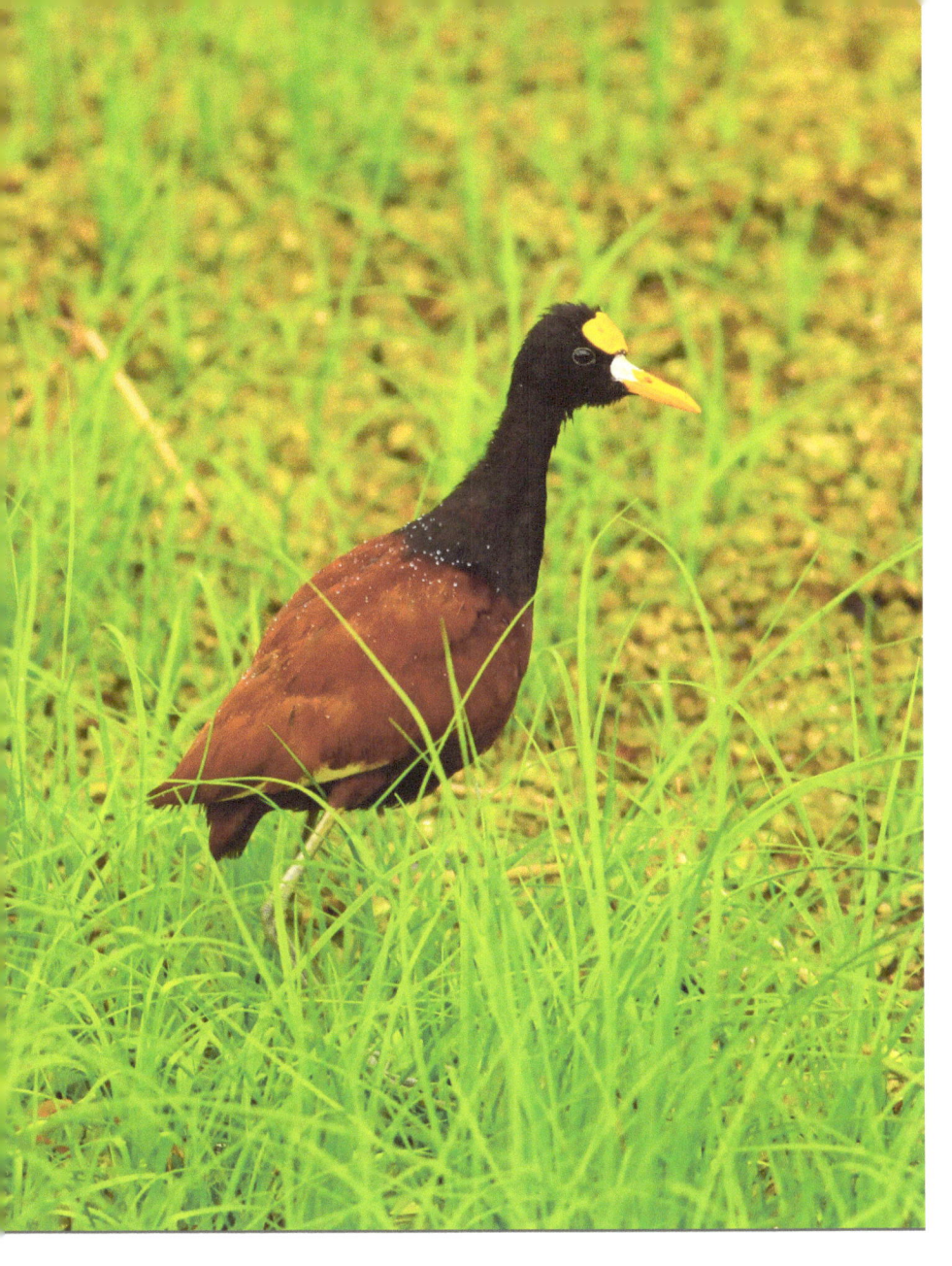

Northern Jacana

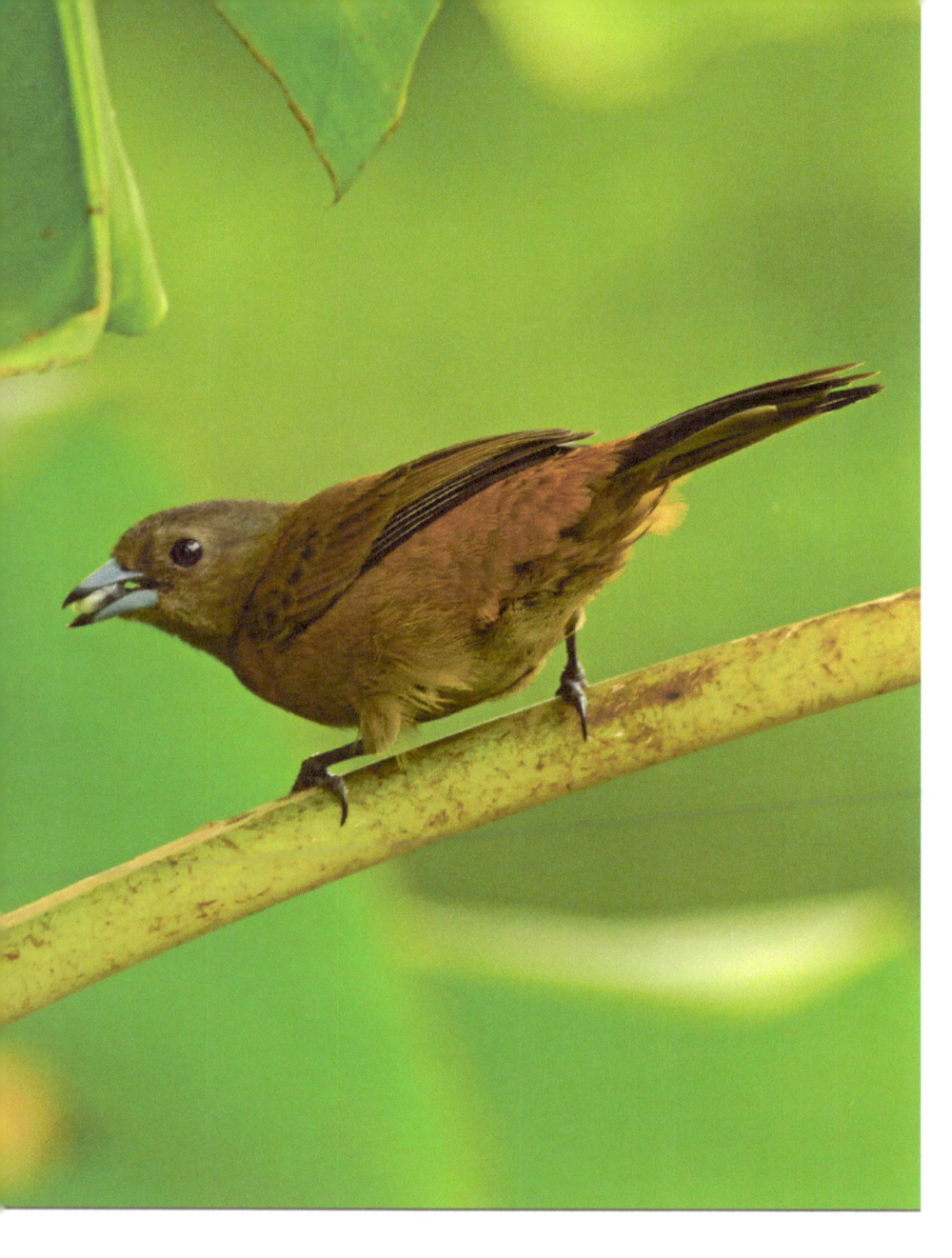

Passerini's Tanager

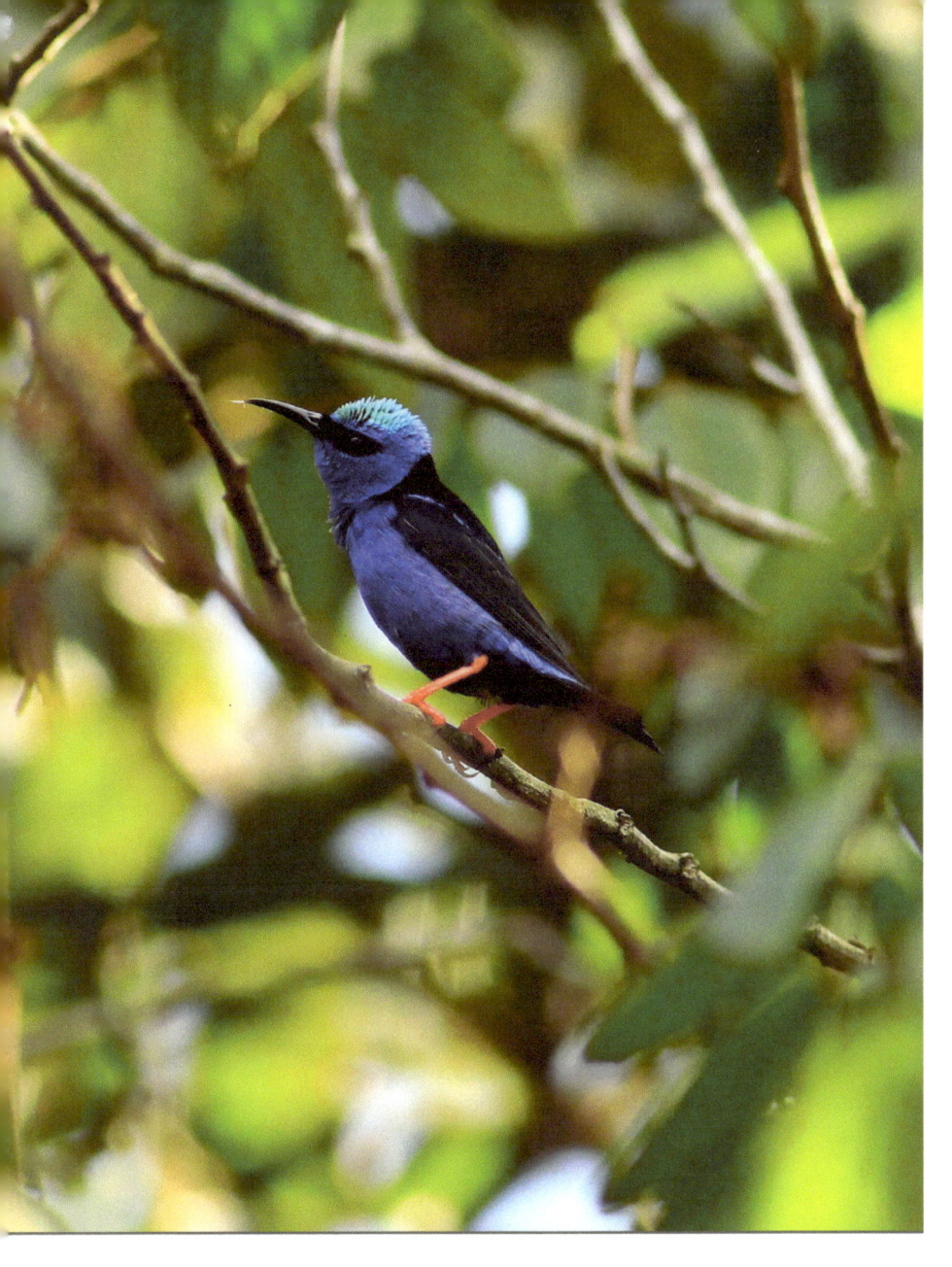

Red-legged Honeycreeper

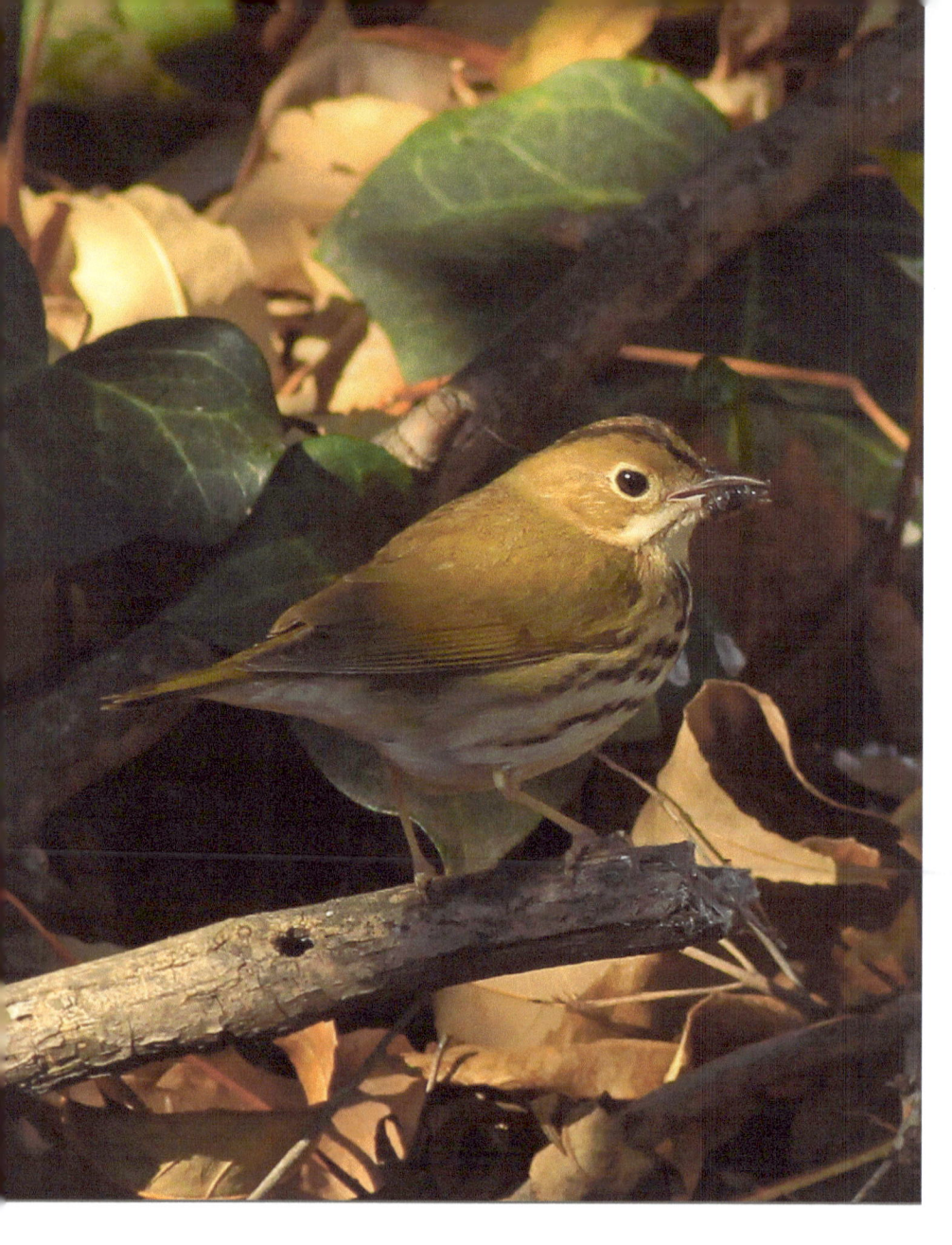

Ovenbird

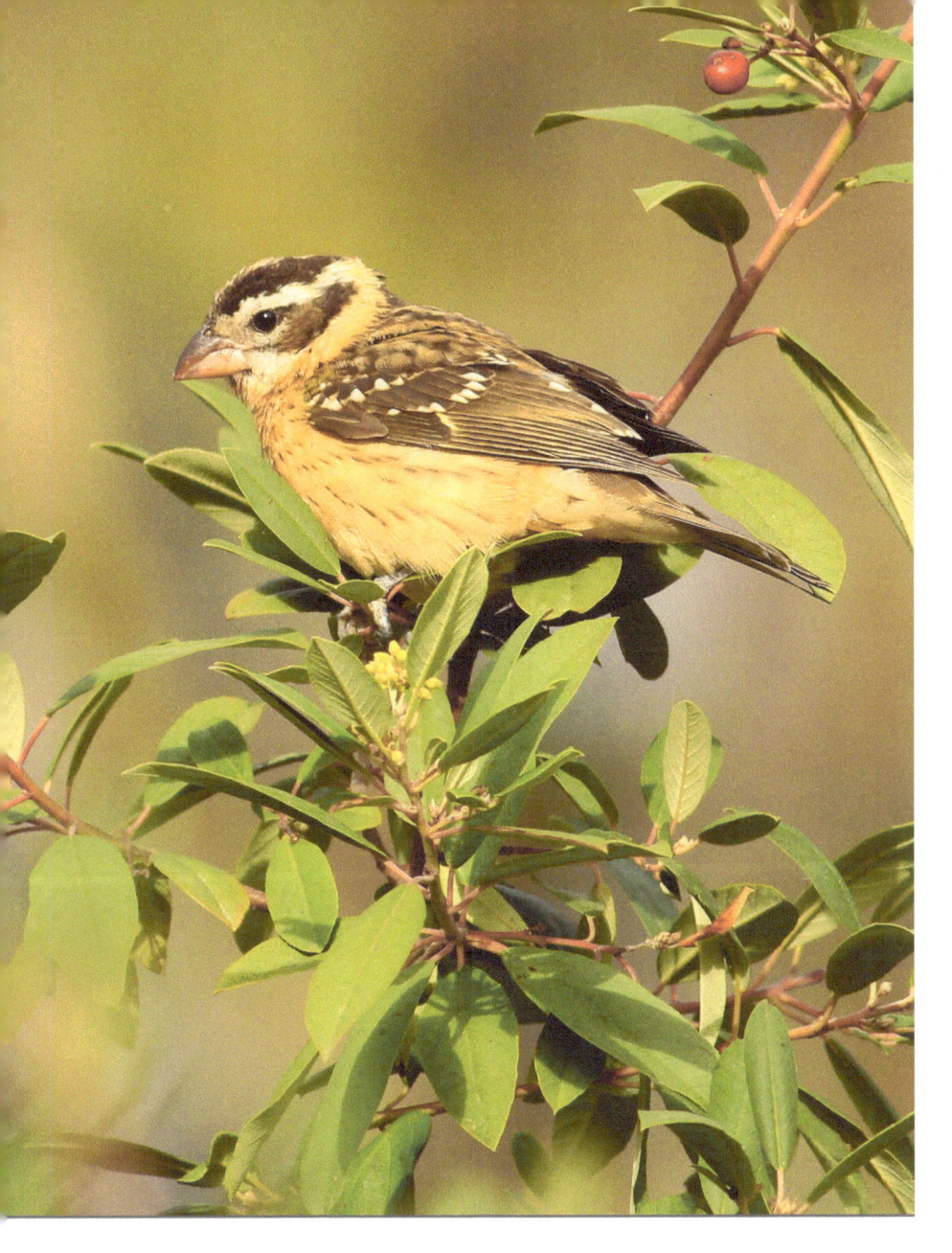

Black-headed Grosbeak

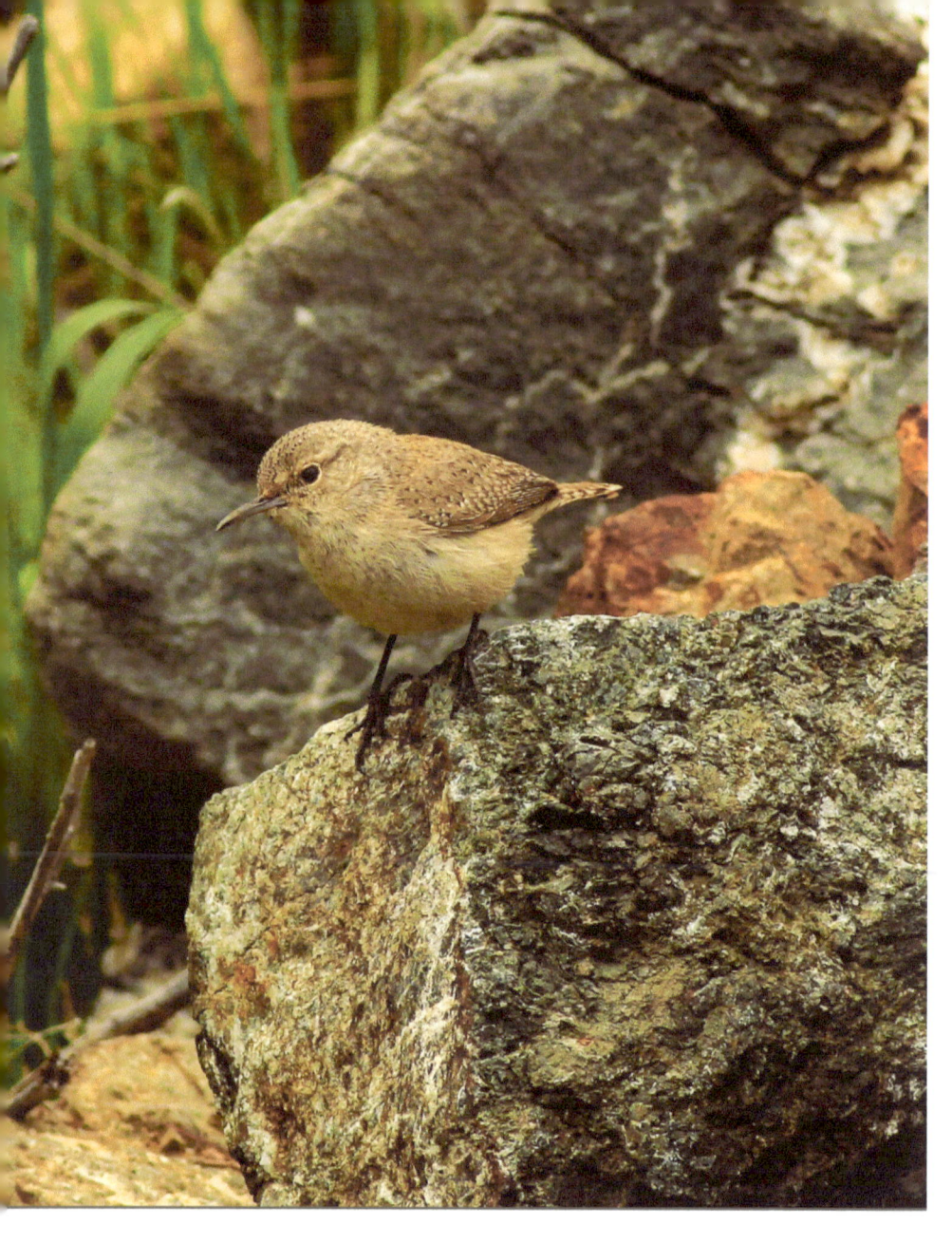

Rock Wren

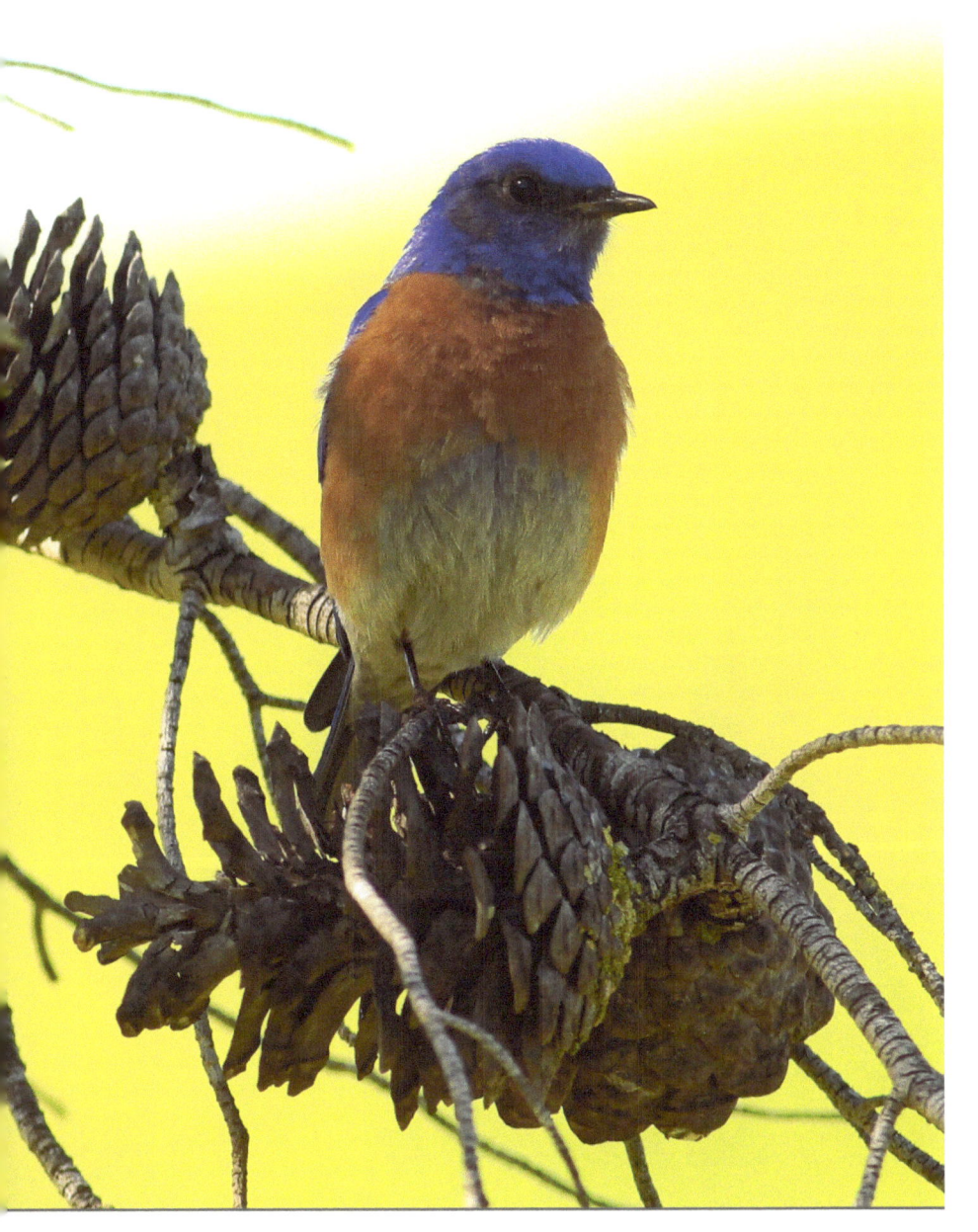

Western Bluebird

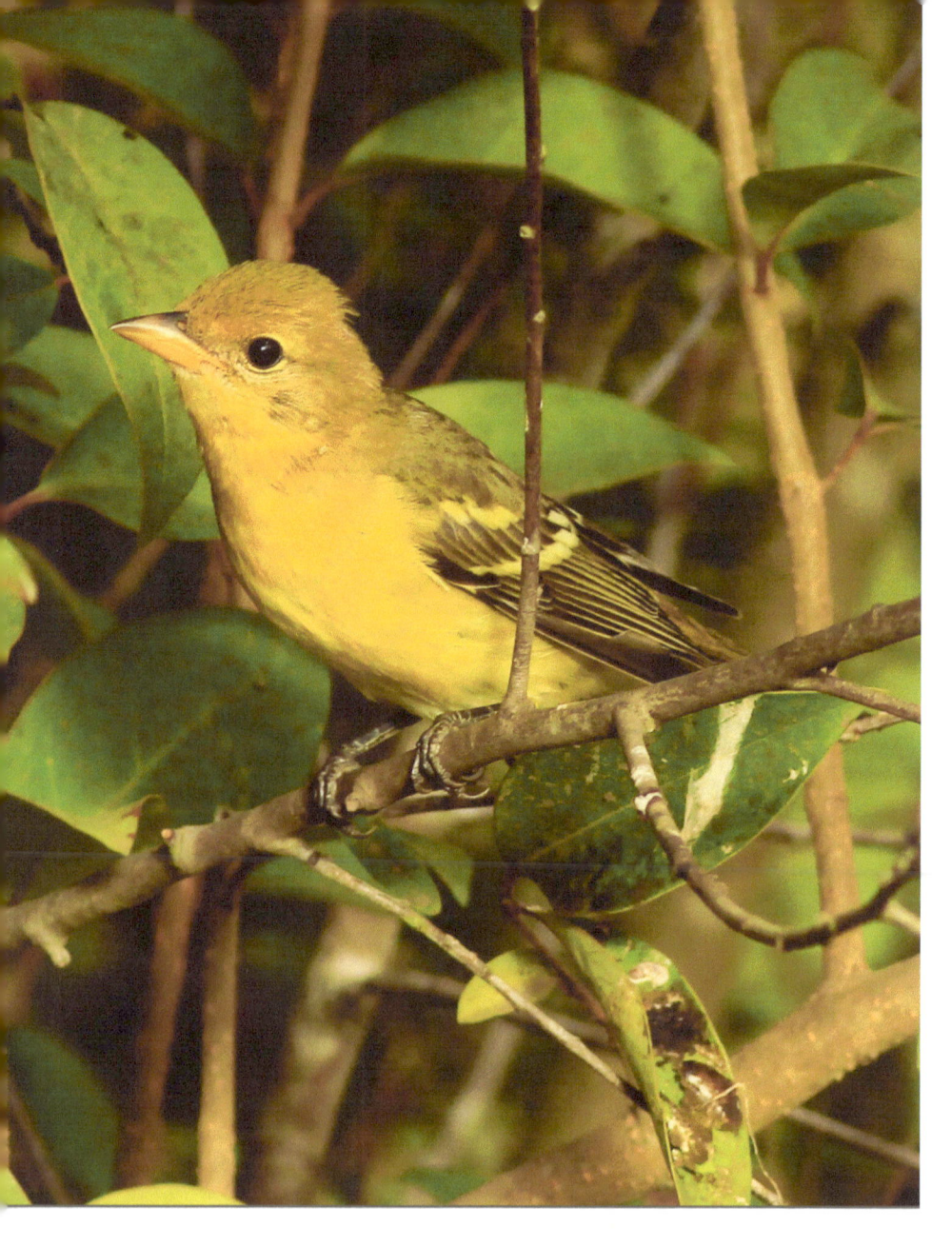

Western Tanager

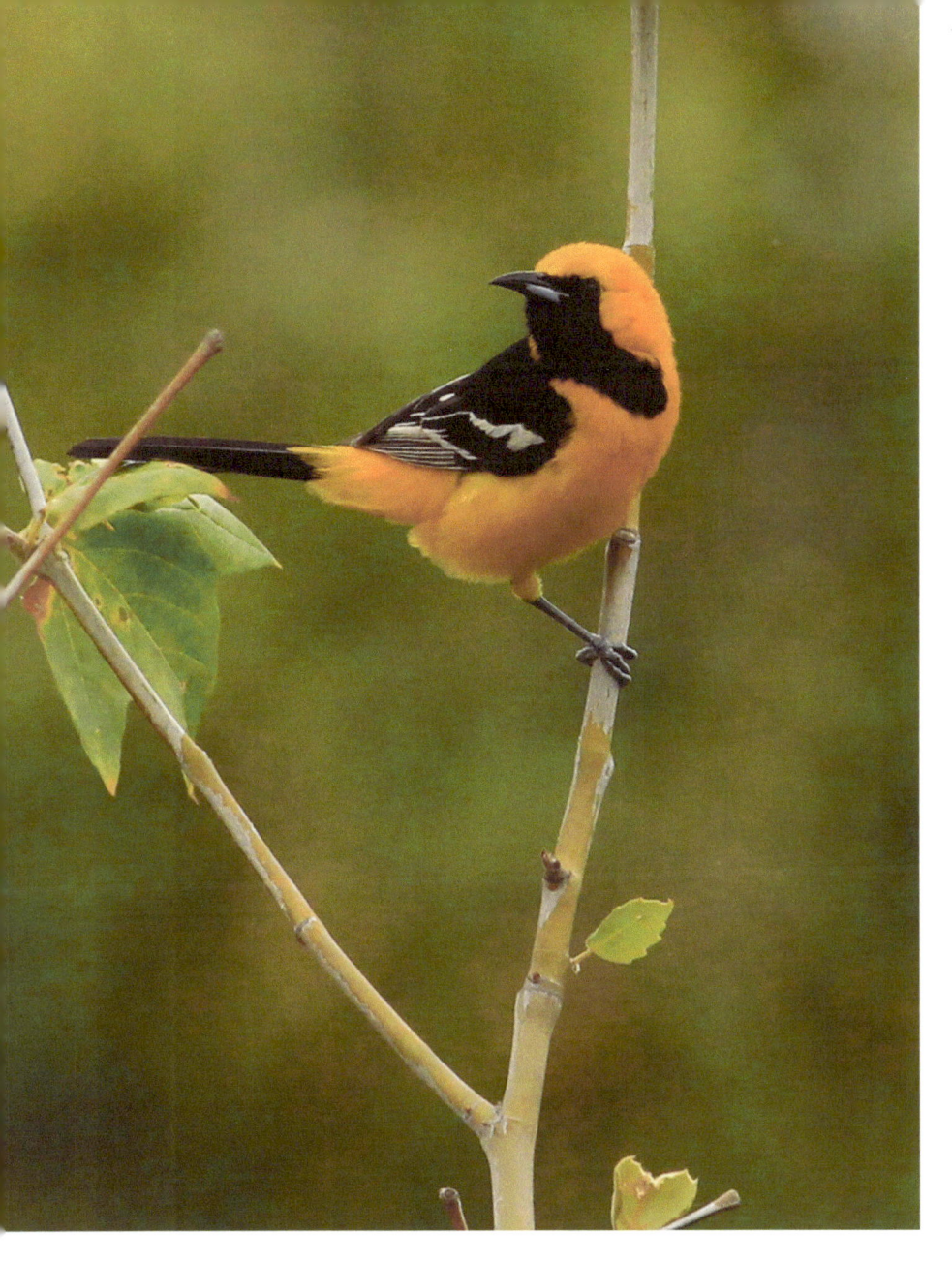

Hooded Oriole

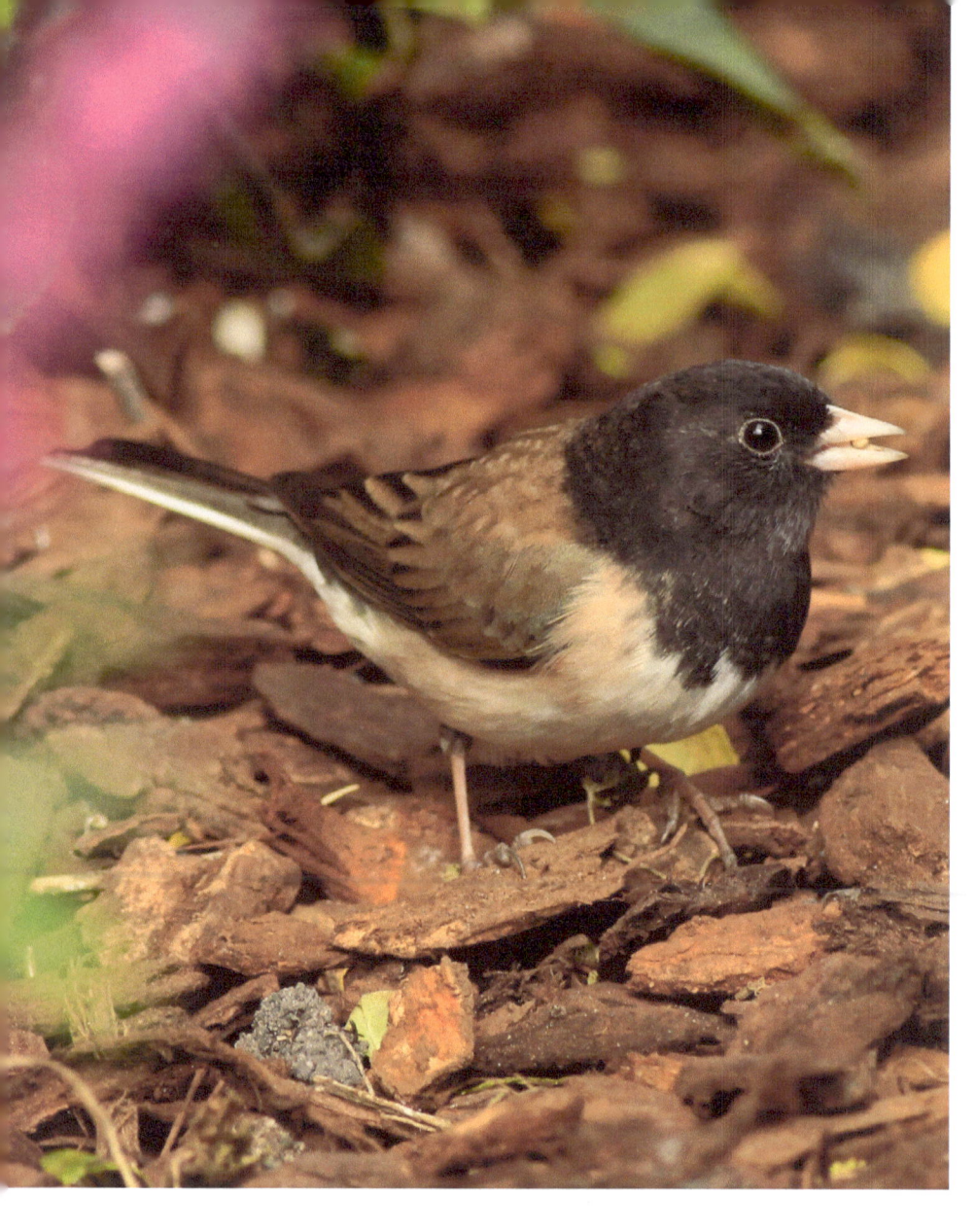

Dark eyed Junco

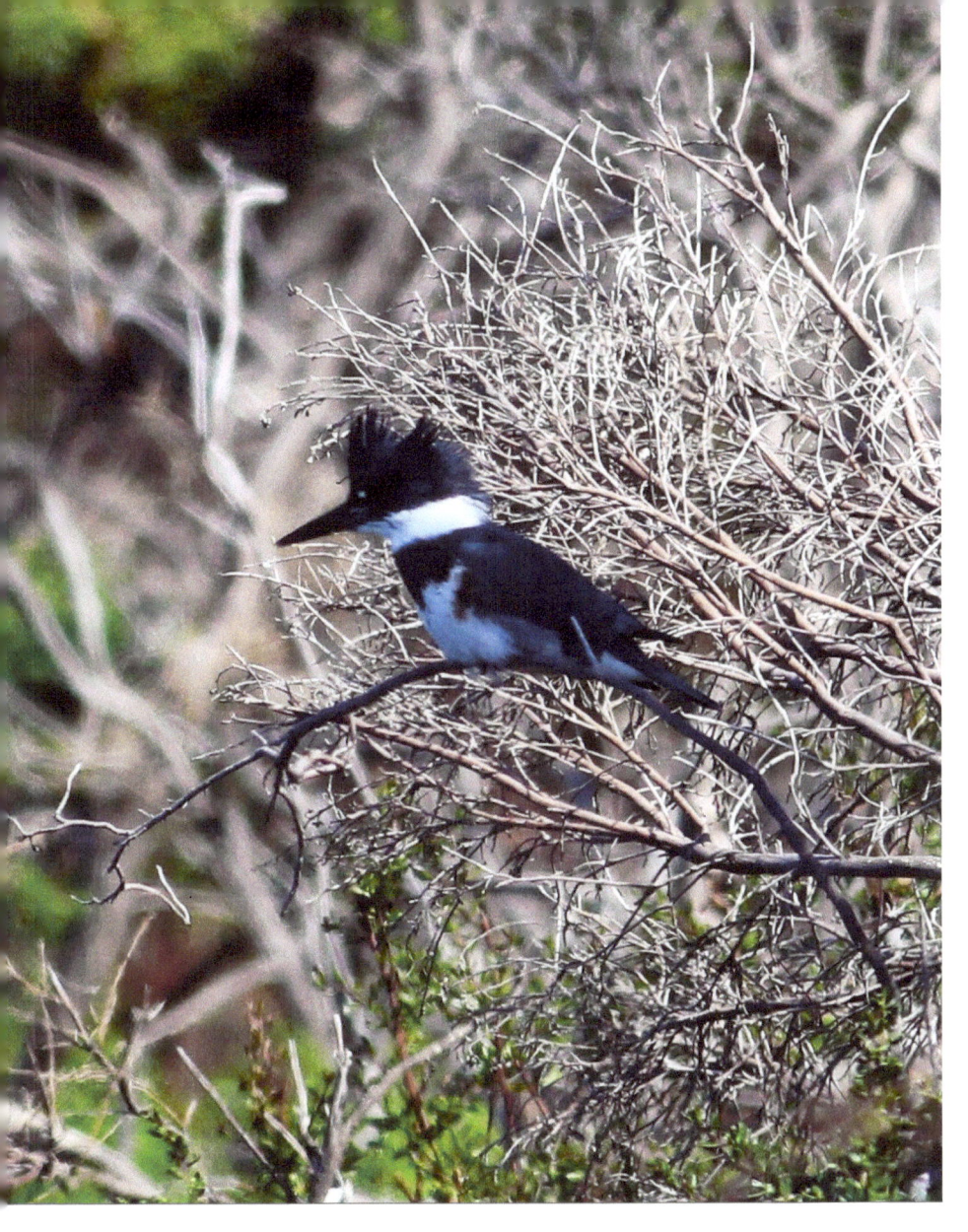

Belted Kingfisher

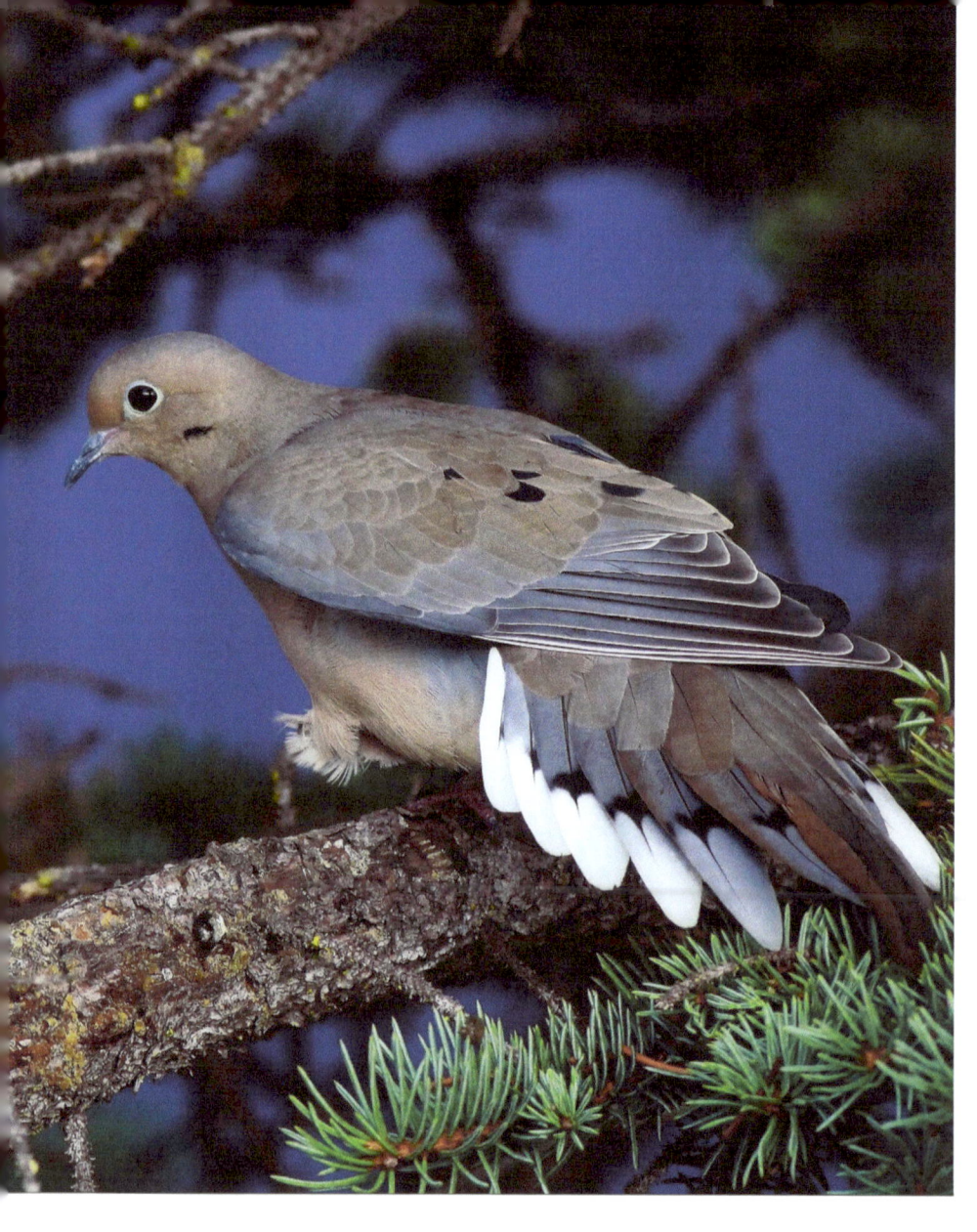

Mourning Dove

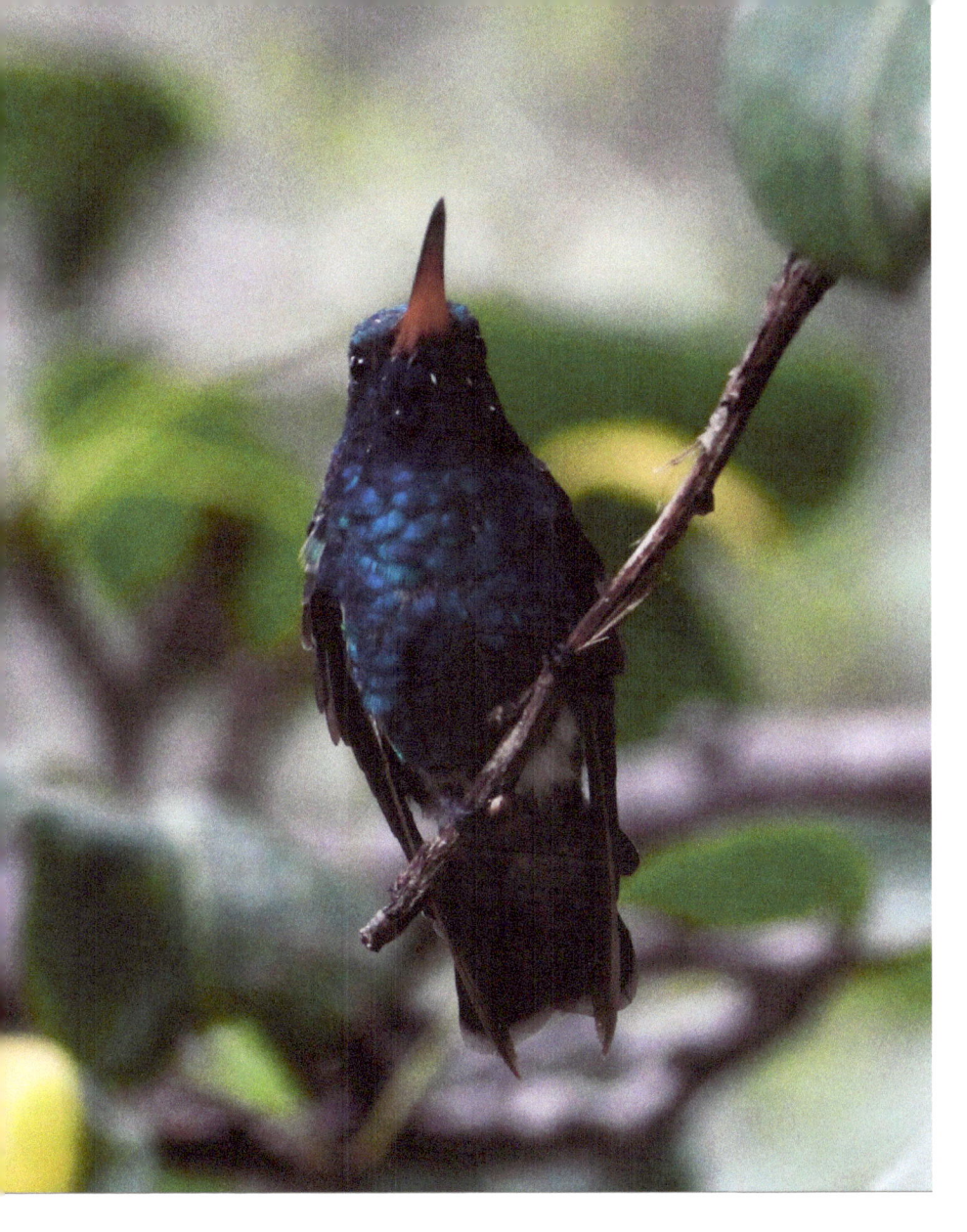

Broad-billed Hummingbird

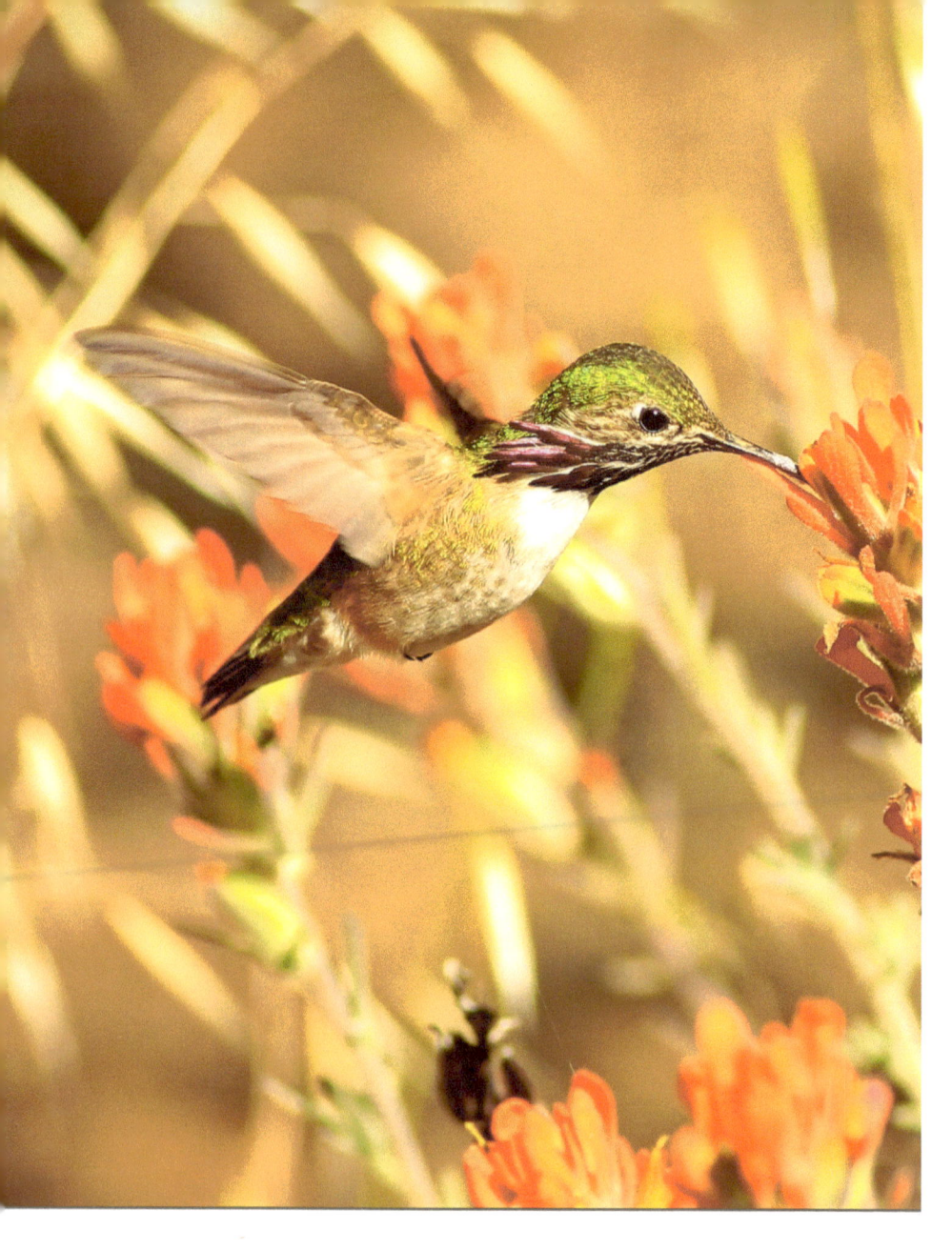

Caliope Hummingbird

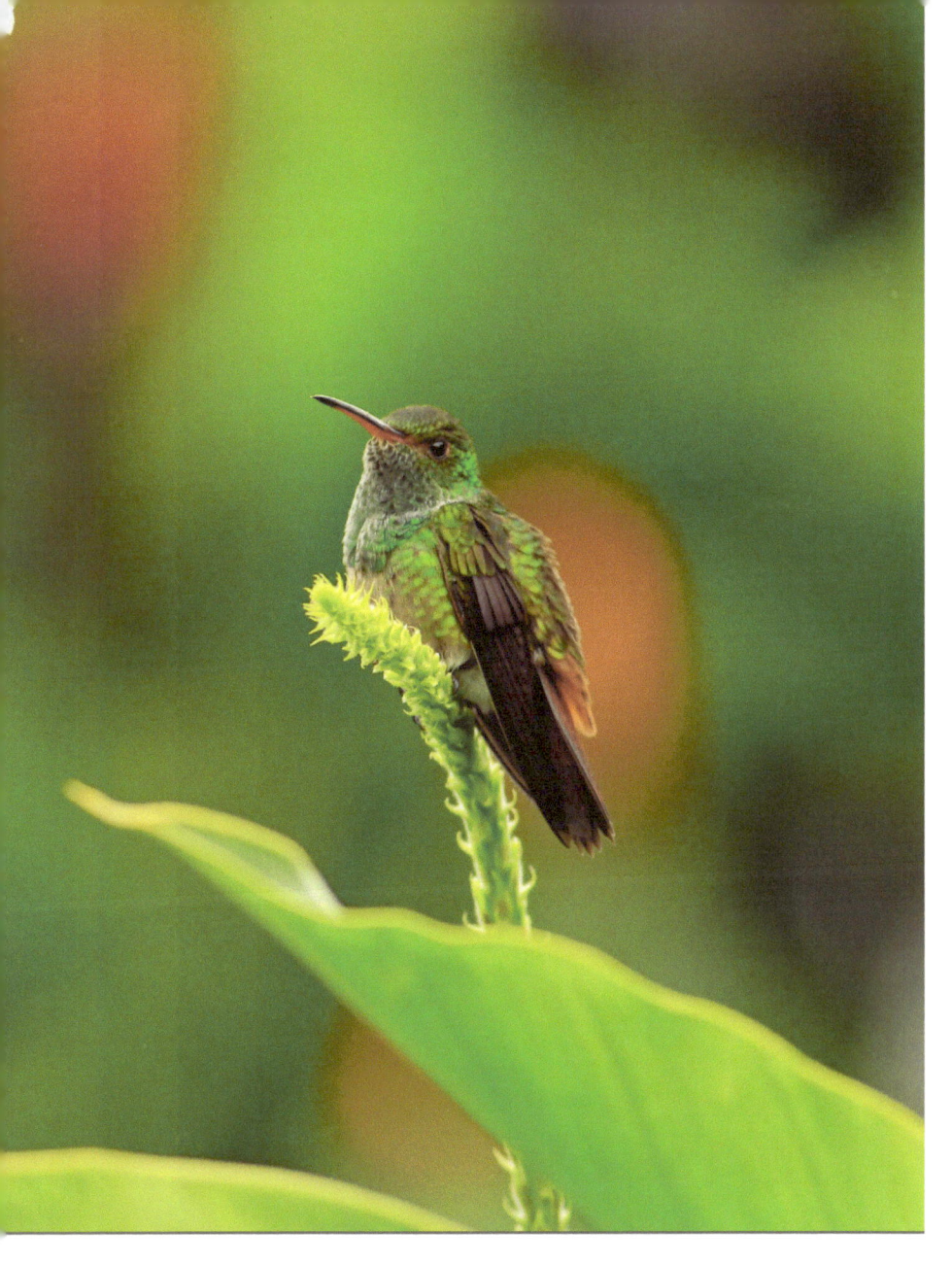

Rufous-tailed Hummingbird

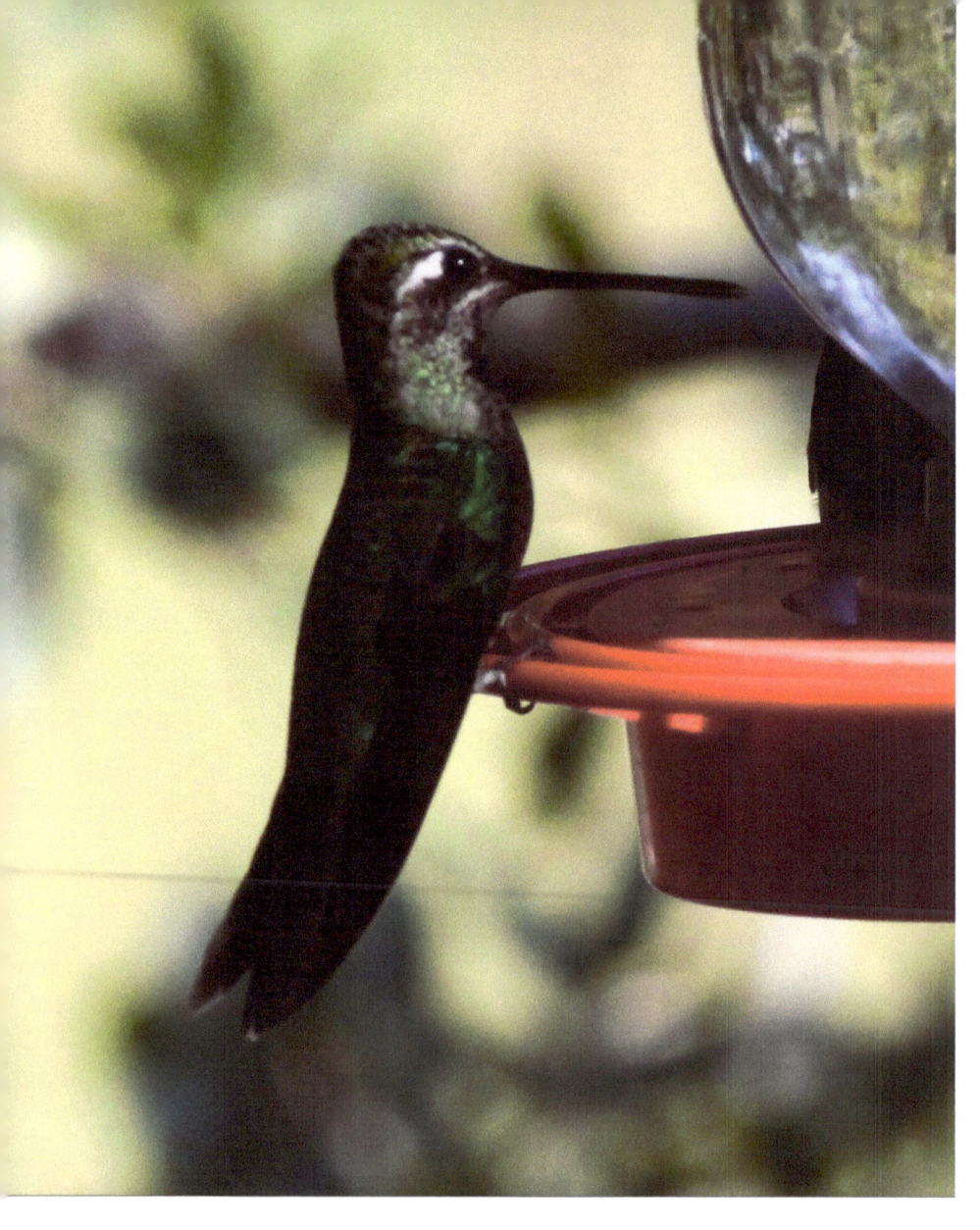

Blue-throated Hummingbird

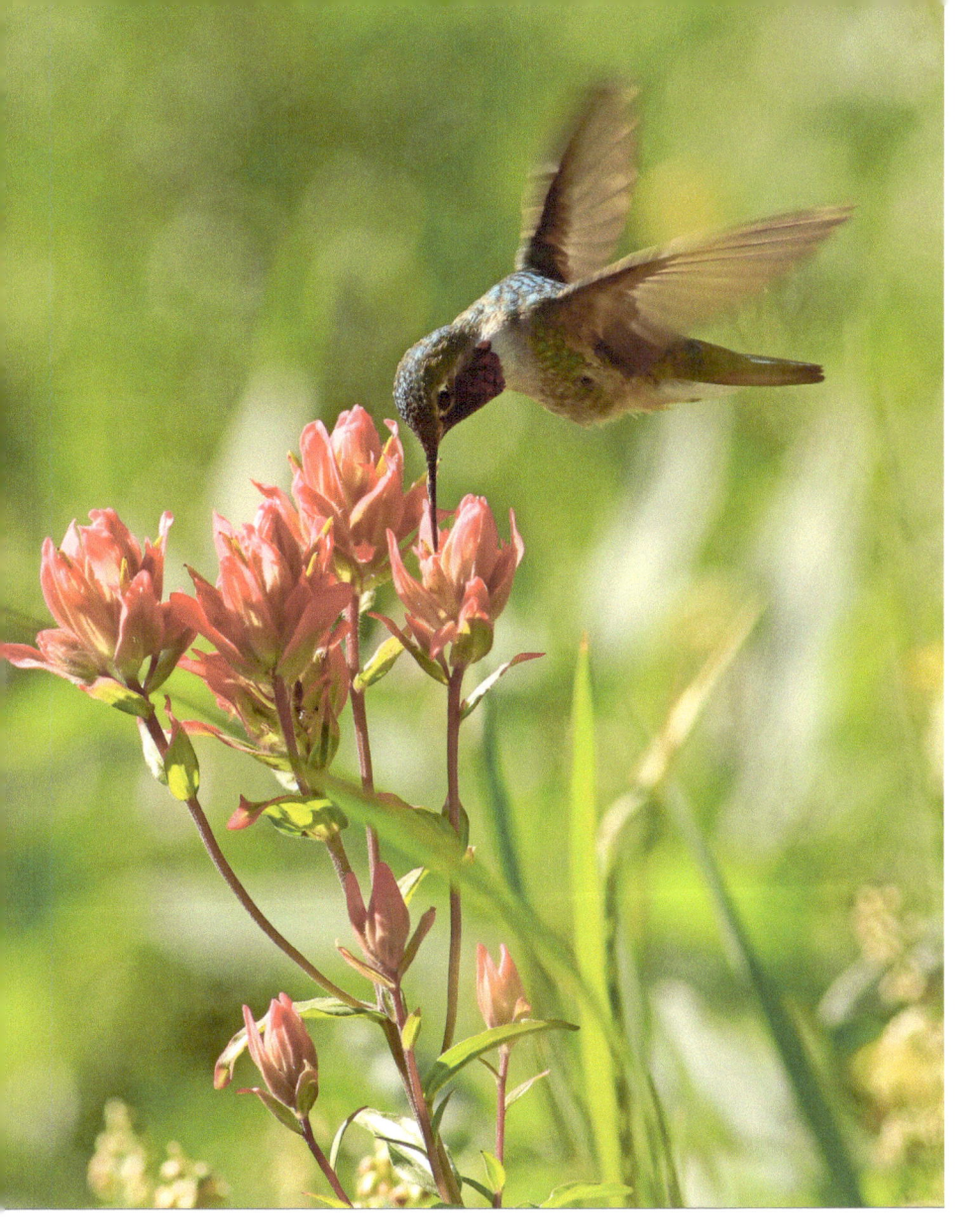

Broad-tailed Hummingbird

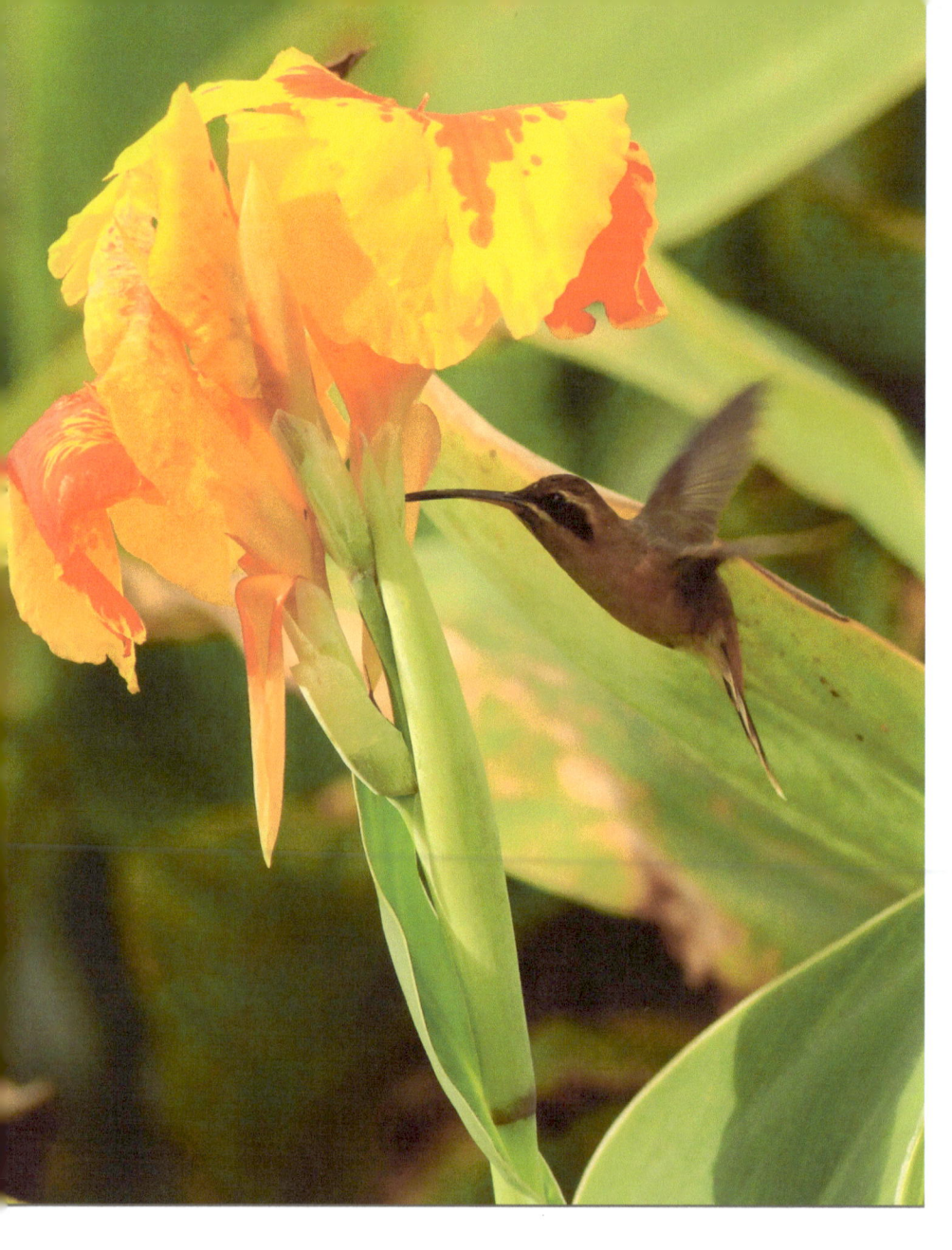

Stripe-throated Hermit Hummingbird

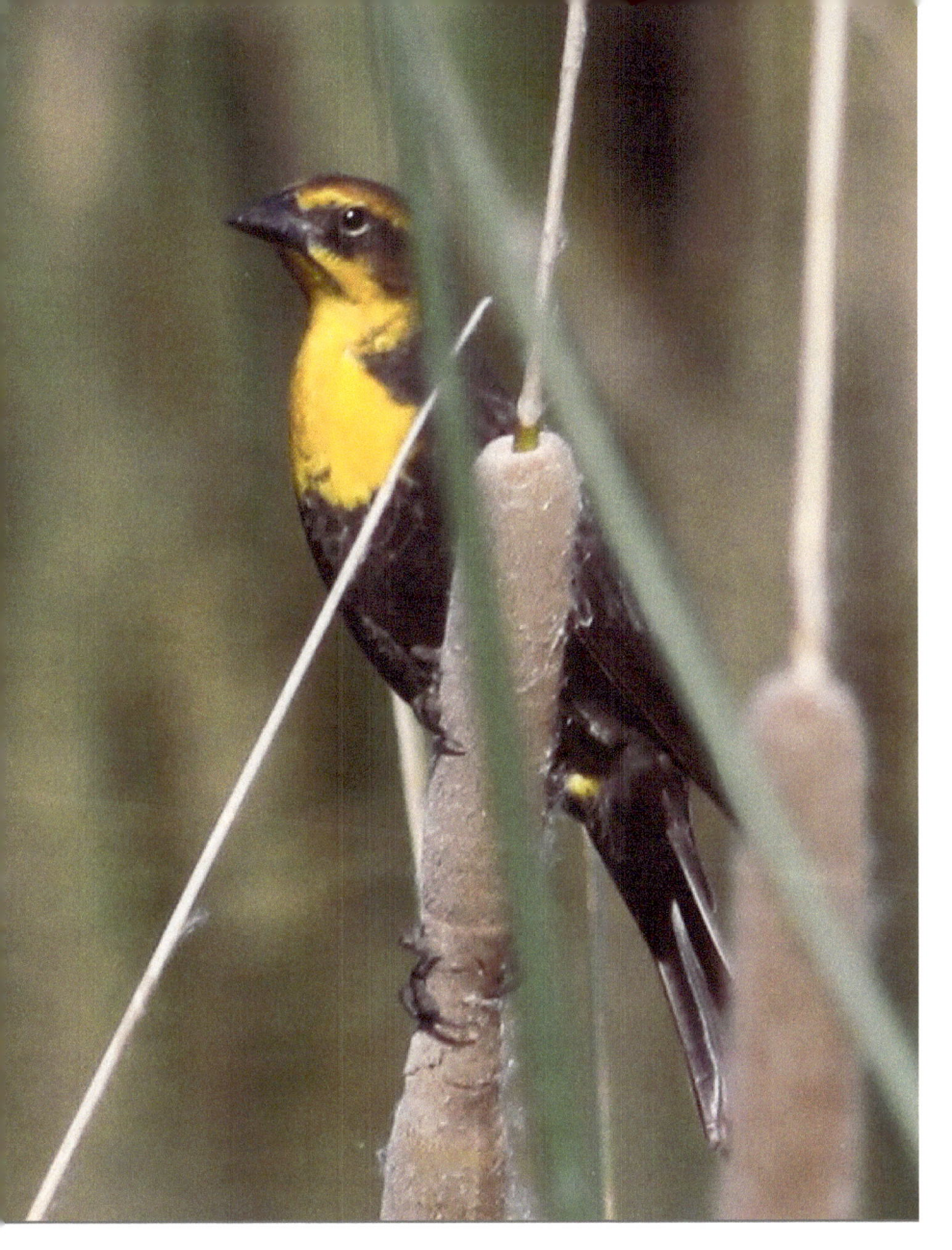

Yellow-headed Blackbird

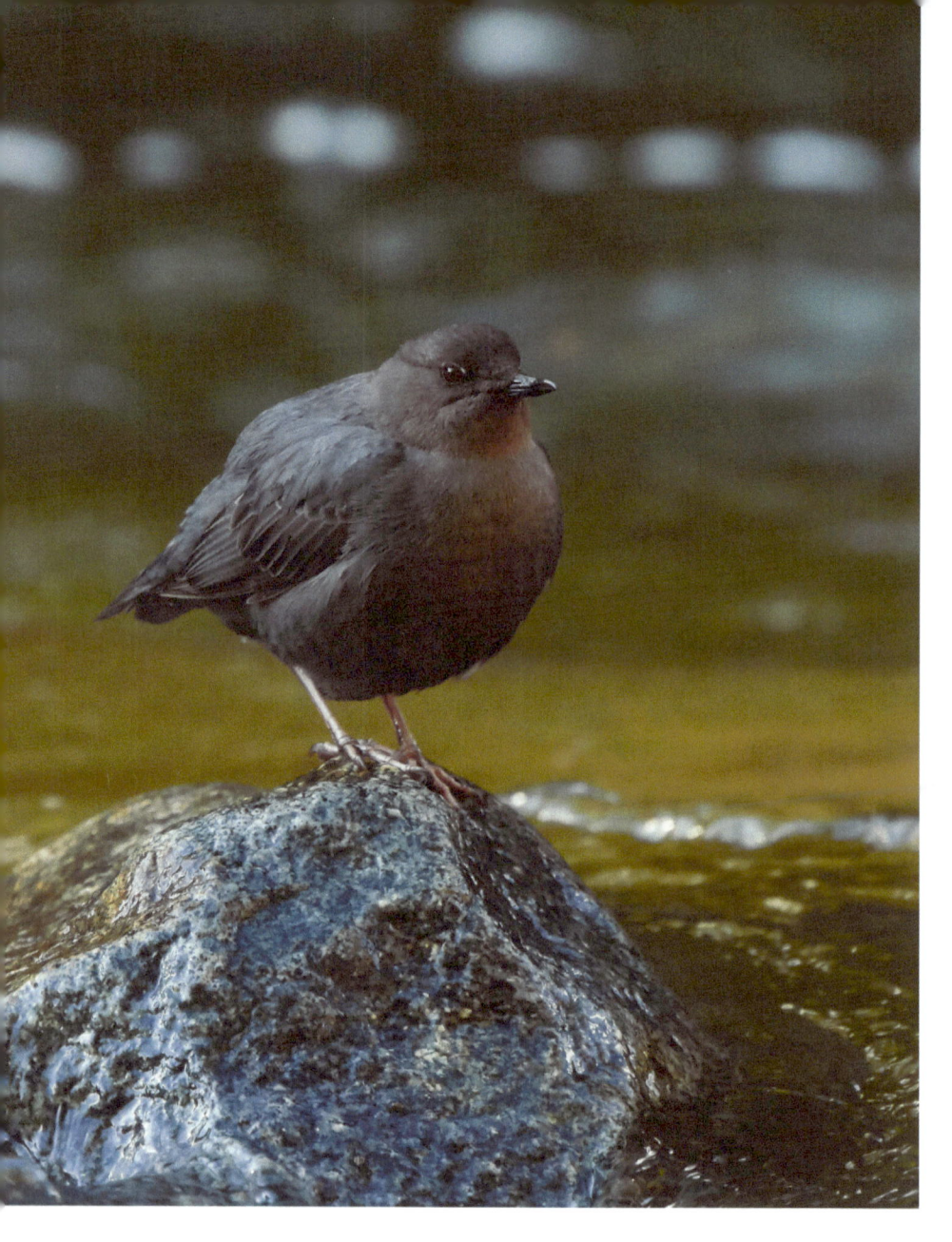

American Dipper

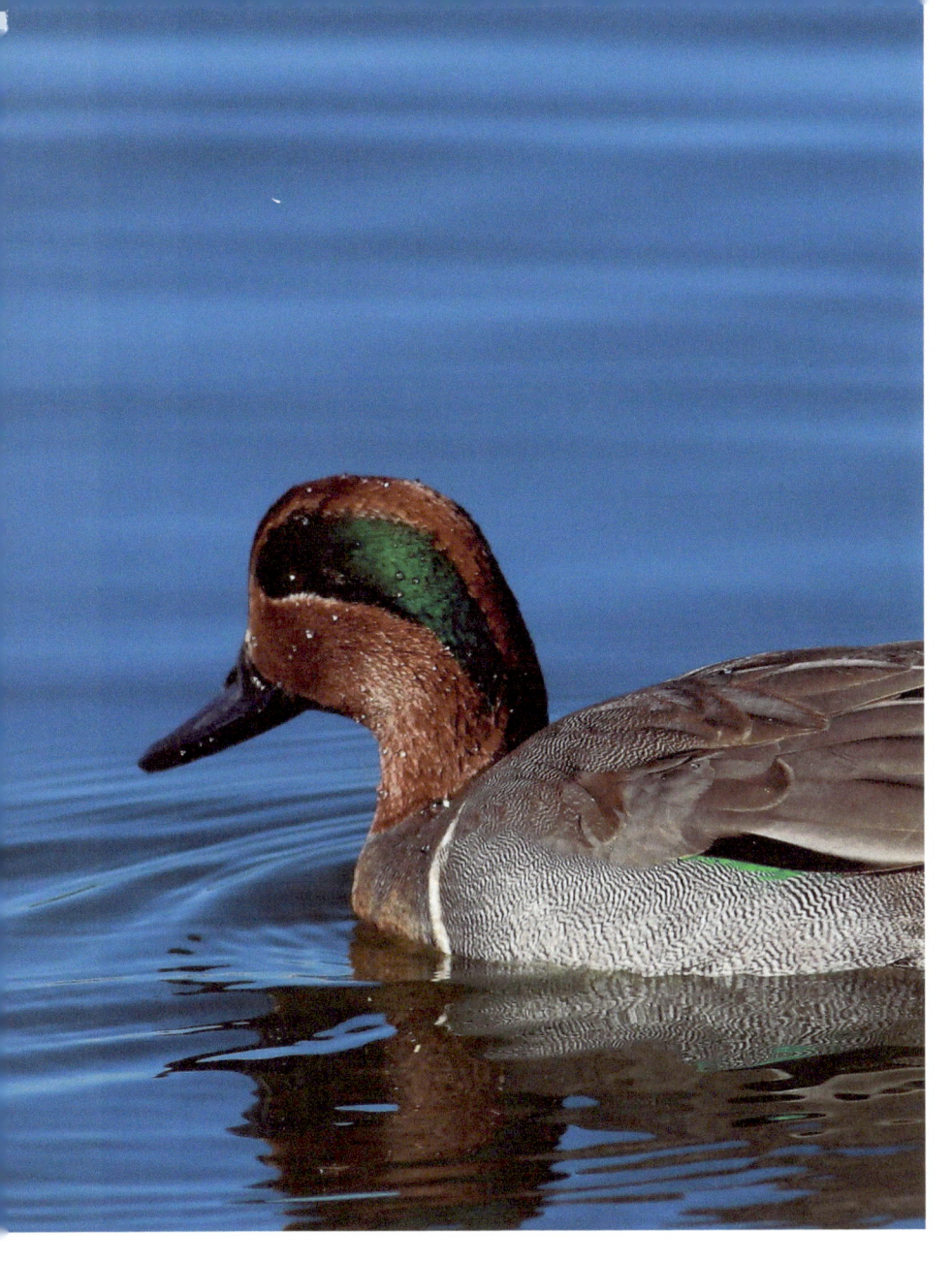

Green-winged Teal

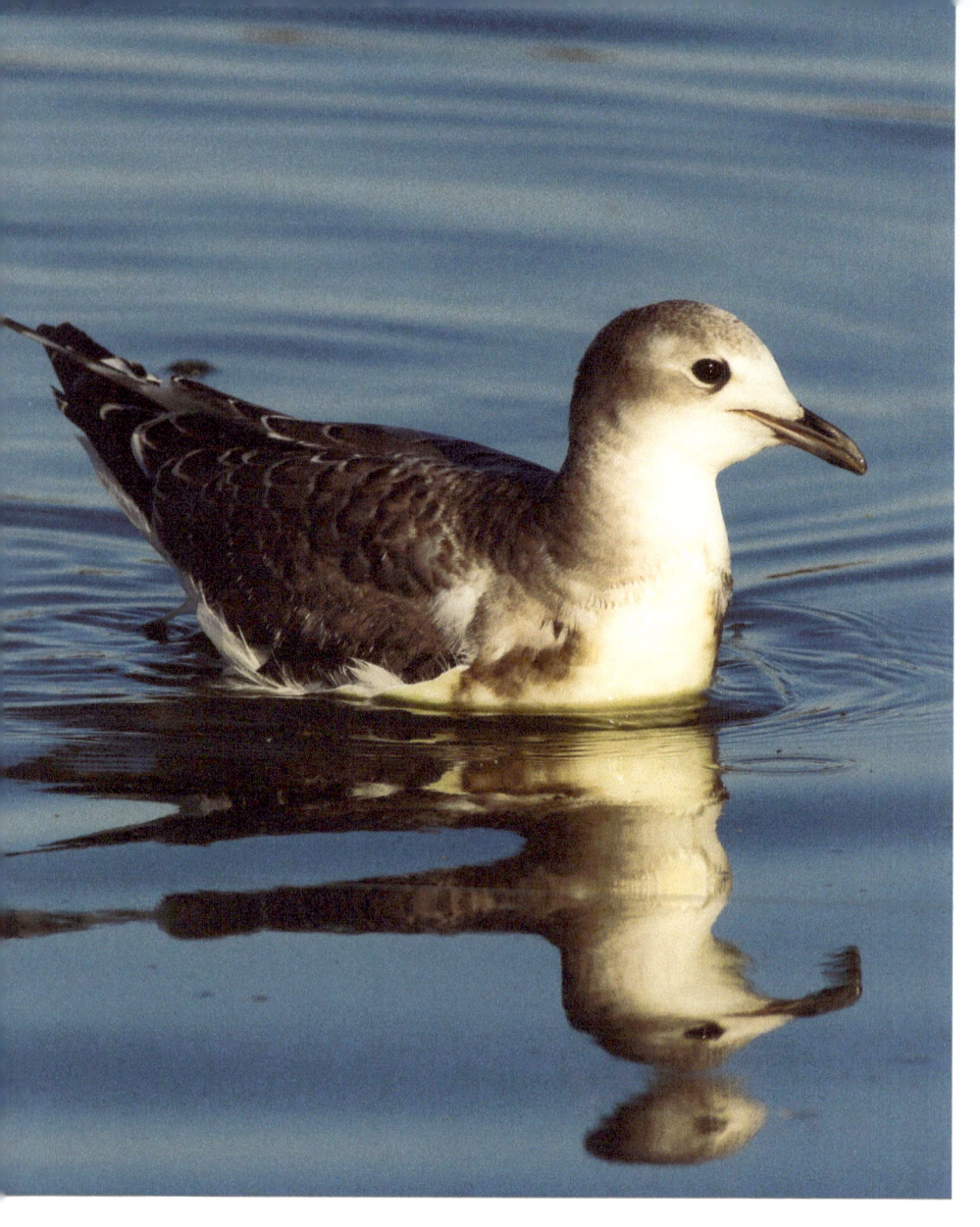

Sabine's Gull

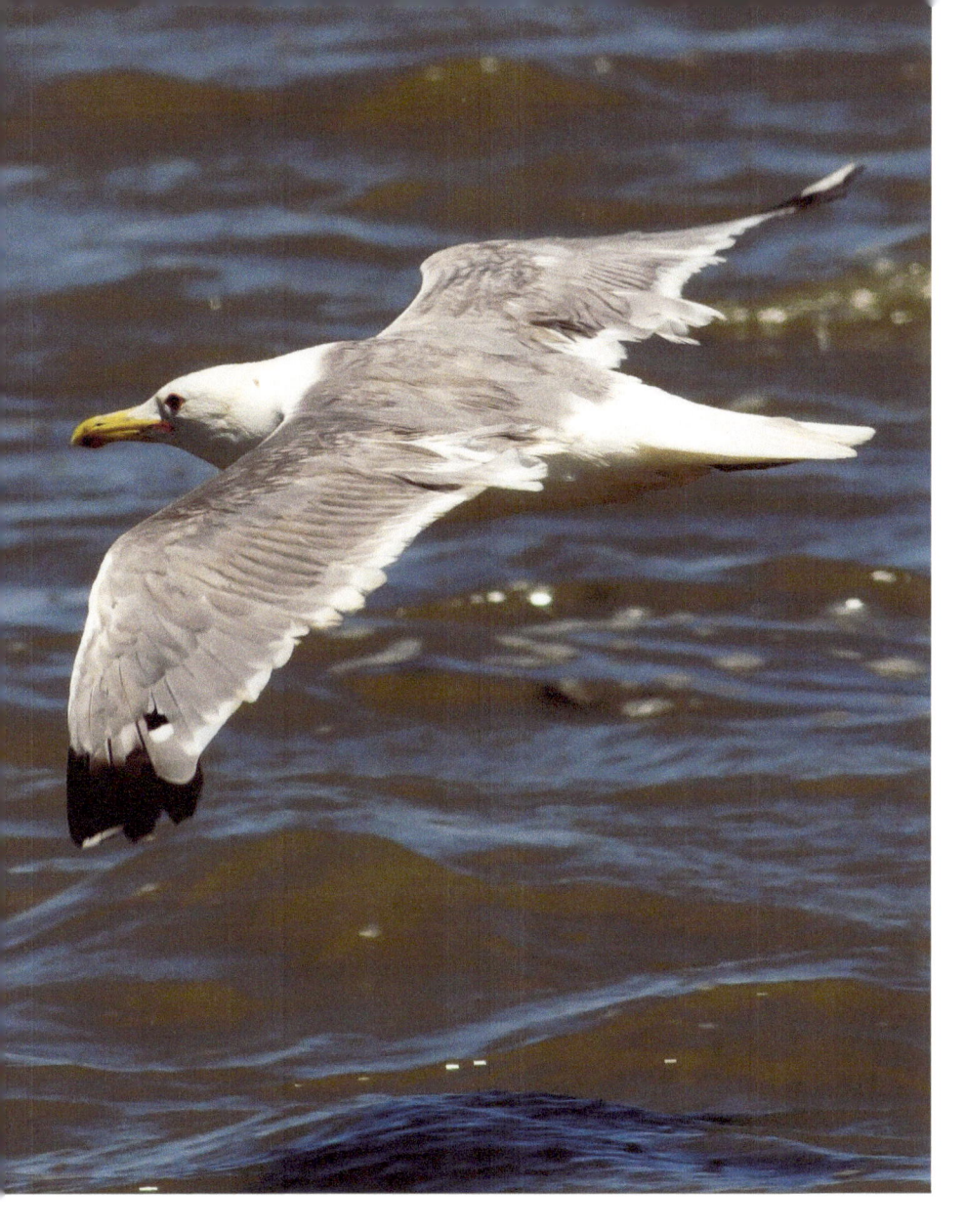

California Gull

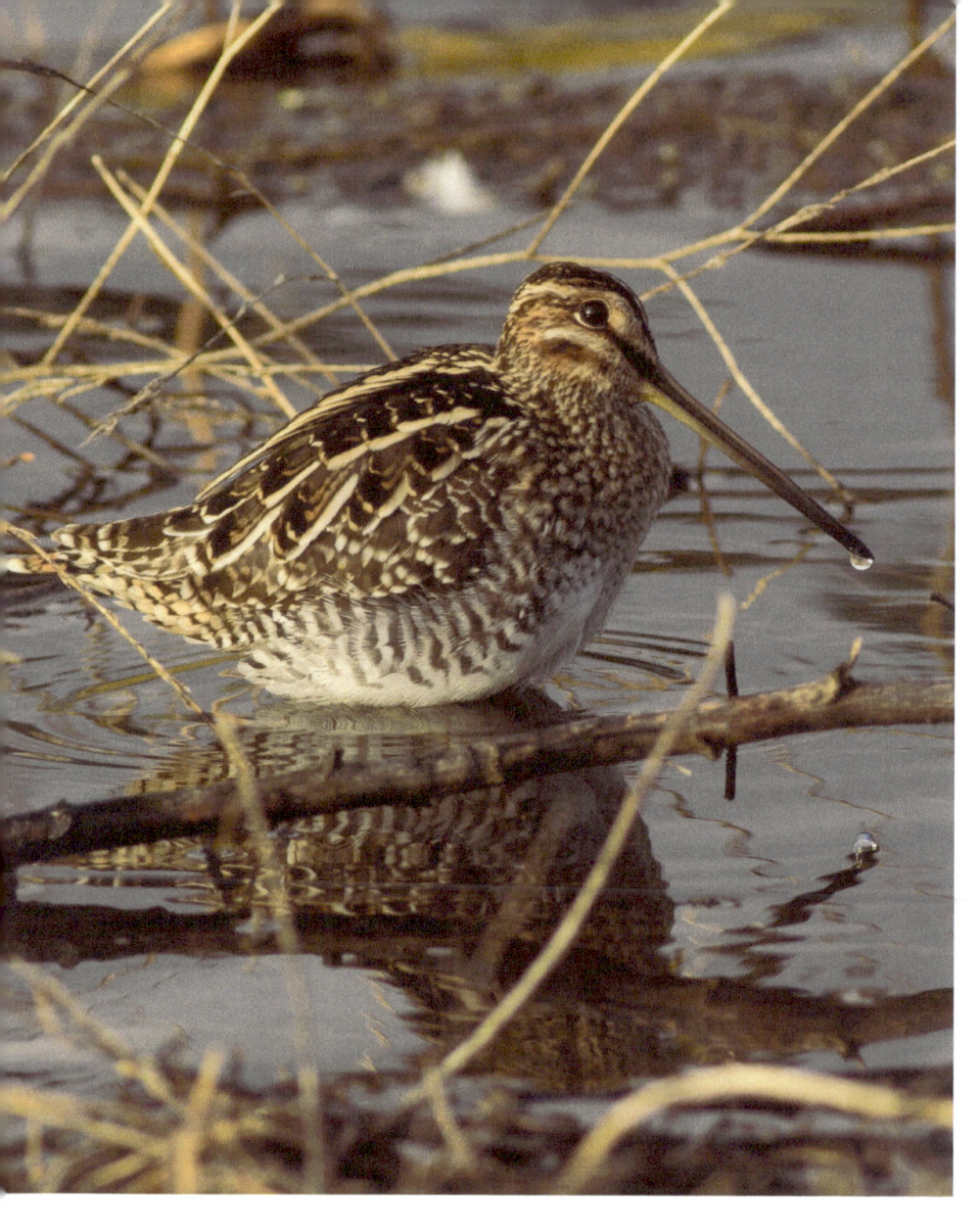

Wilson's Snipe

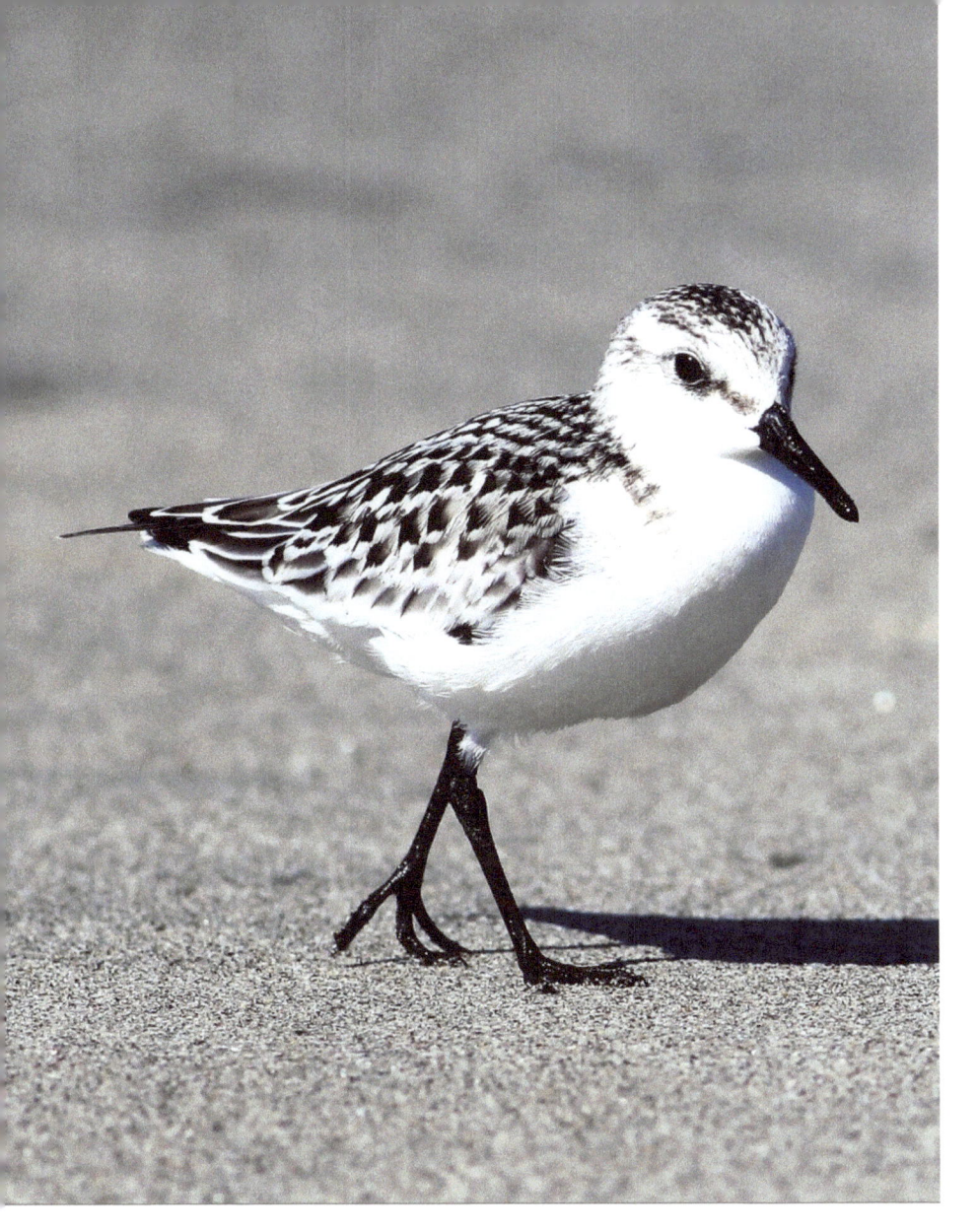

Sanderling

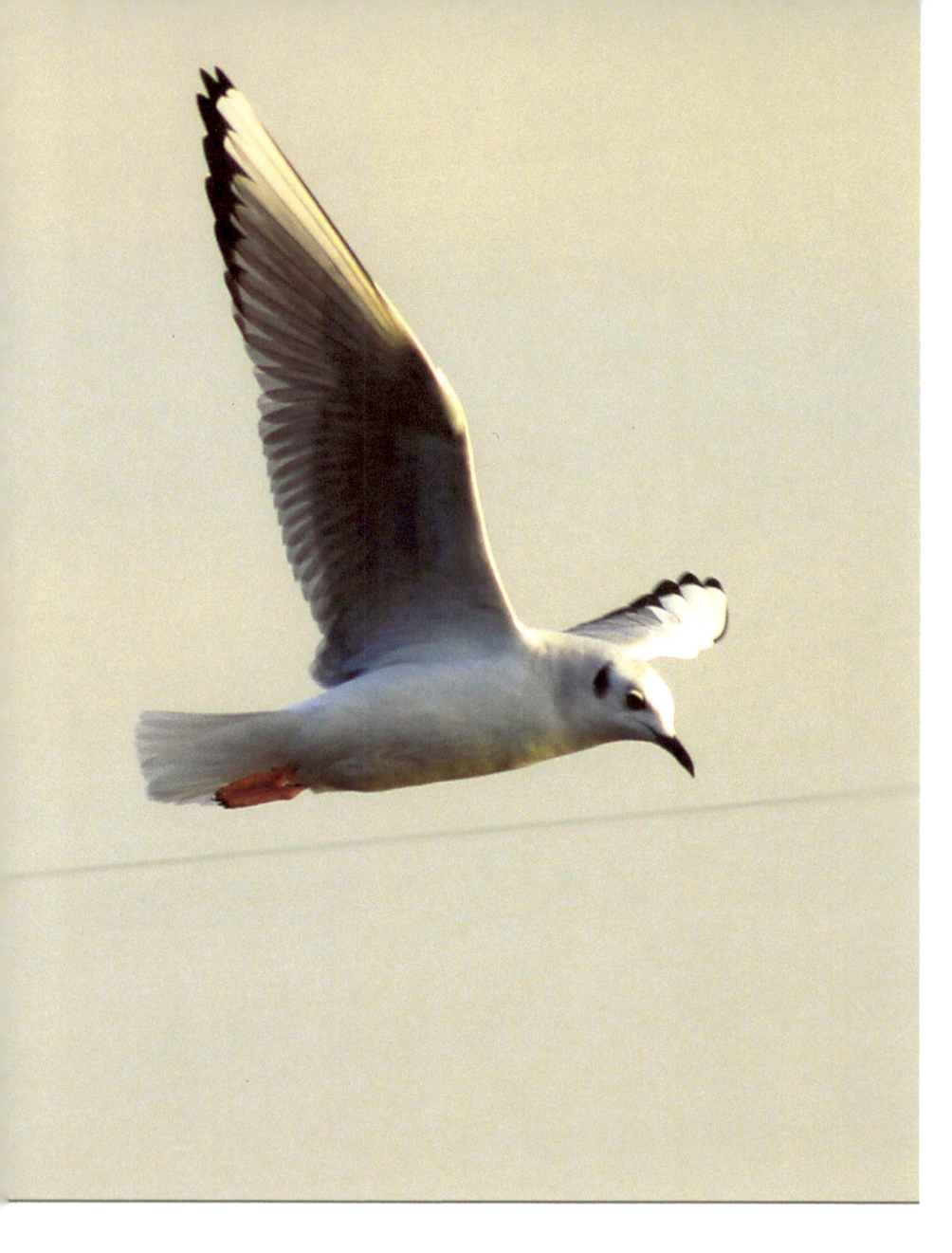

Bonaparte's Gull

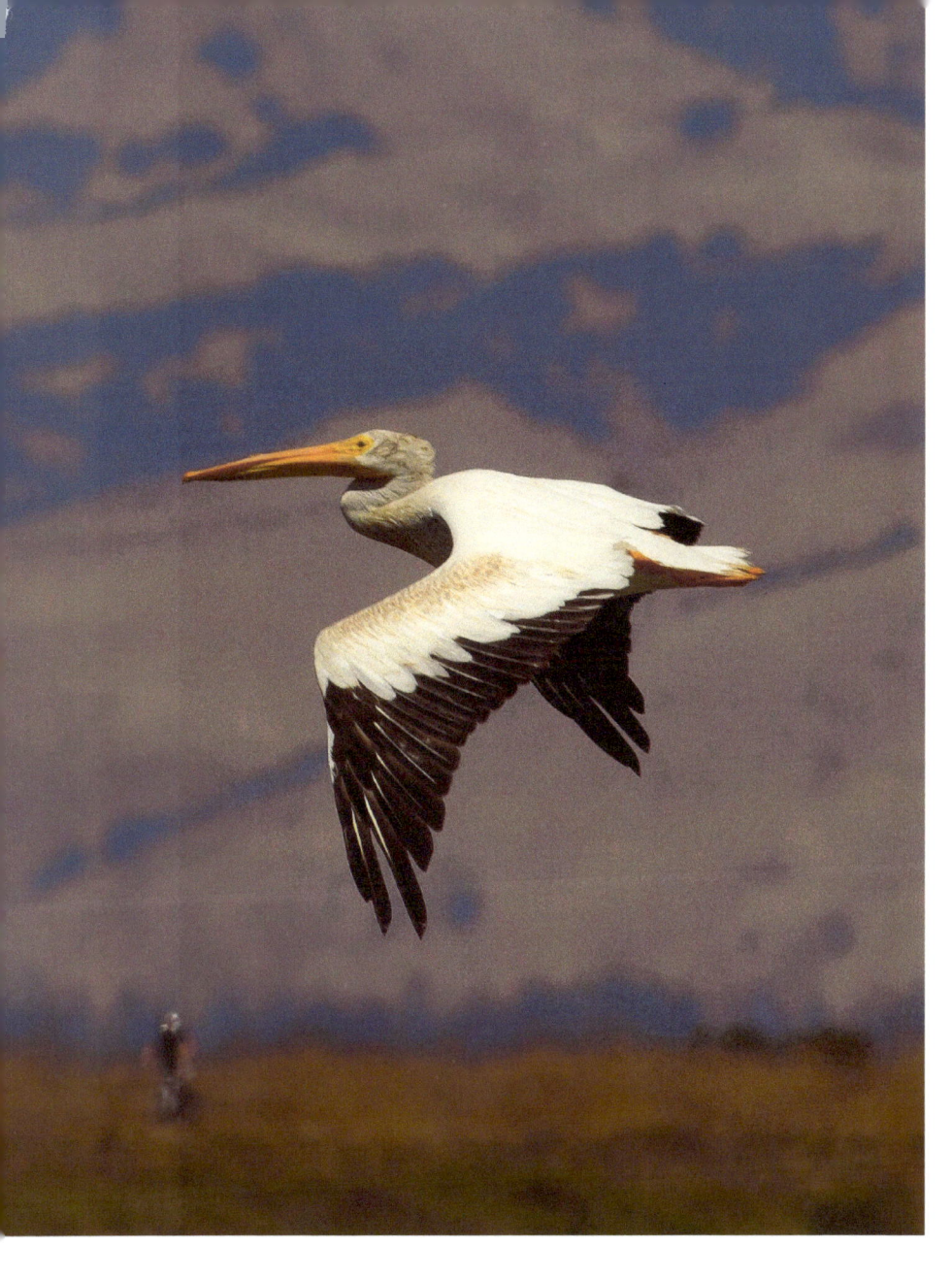

White Pelican

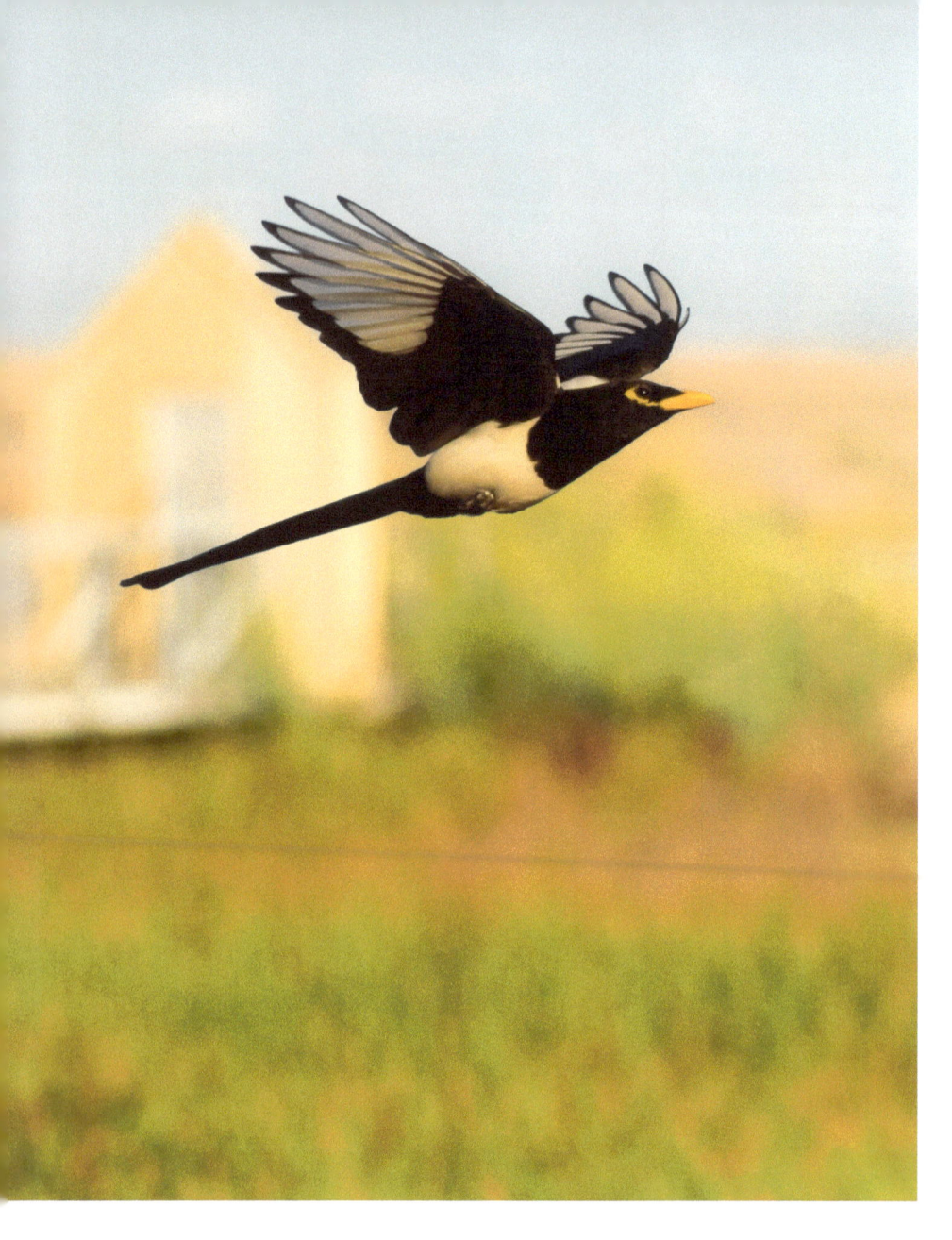

Yellow-billed Magpie

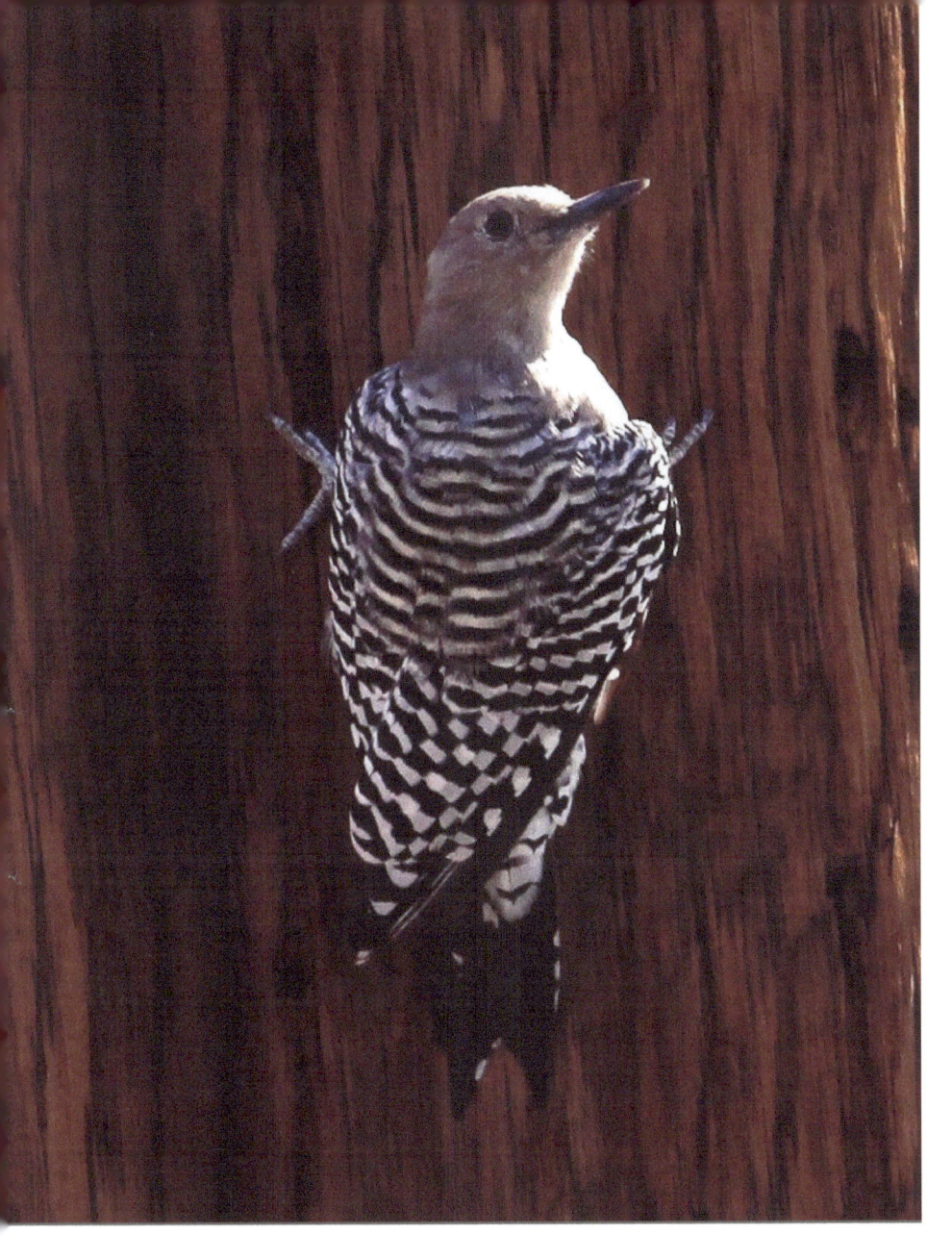

Gila Woodpecker

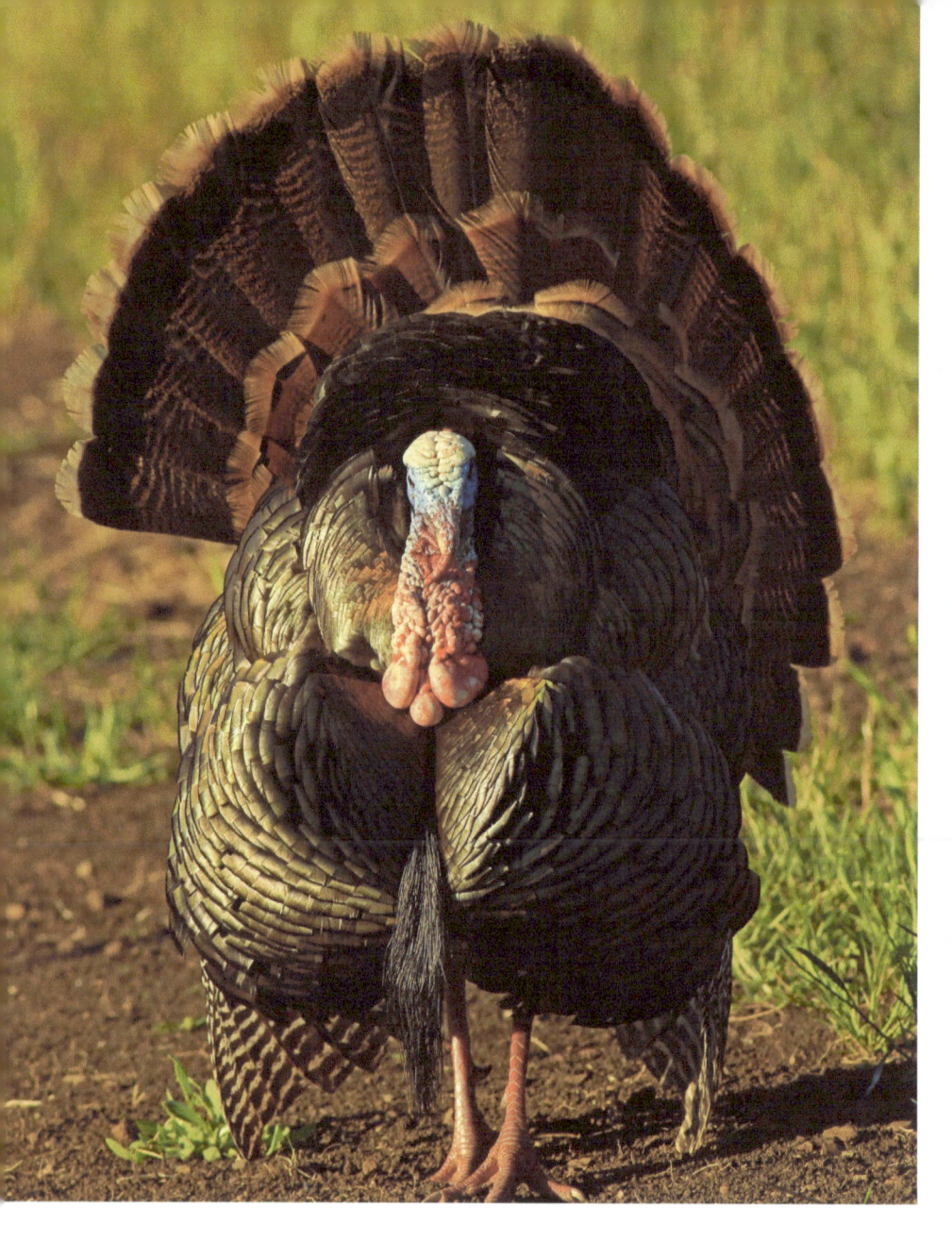

Turkey

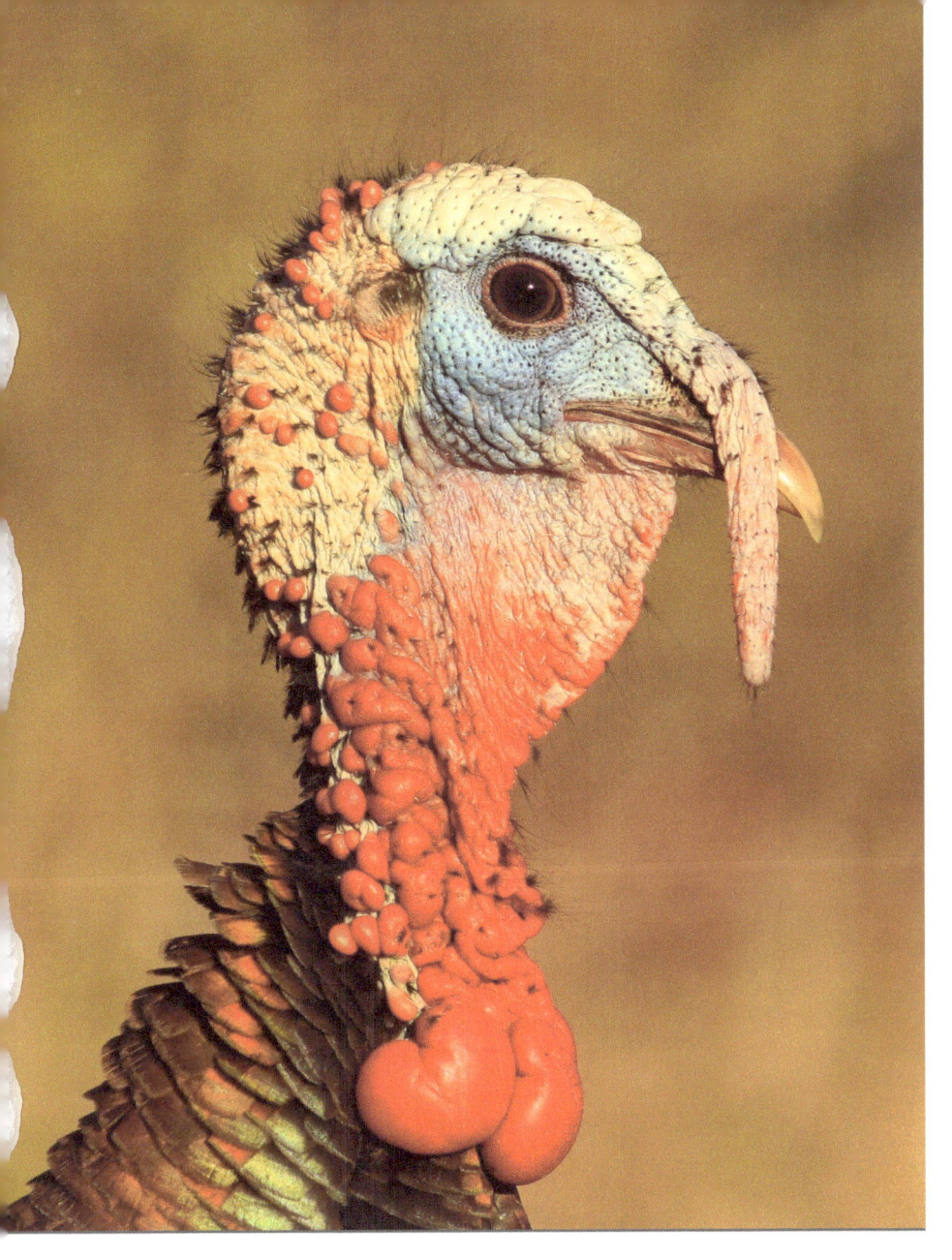

Turkey